SPEECHES
ON
INDIAN AFFAIRS

SPEECHES
ON
INDIAN AFFAIRS

JOHN MORLEY

GYAN

Published by

Gyan Publishing House
5, Ansari Road
Daryaganj, New Delhi-110002
Phone: 011-47034999, 9811692060
E-mail: books@gyanbooks.com

Distribution Network
gyanbooks.com
India, USA, Canada, UK, Australia

ISBN: 978-93-6920-279-9 (PB)

First Published, 1920

2nd Impression 2025

Printed at: Gyan Press, Delhi.

SPEECHES ON INDIAN AFFAIRS
Author: JOHN MORLEY

SPEECHES

ON

INDIAN AFFAIRS

BY

JOHN MORLEY

G. A. NATESAN & CO.
MADRaS.

NOTE.

This is the second and up-to-date edition of Lord Morley's Speeches and Writings on Indian affairs. At the moment when the question of Self-Government for India is being keenly discussed on all sides, Lord Morley's Speeches on Indian Reforms, particularly those made in the House of Commons and in the House of Lords in his capacity as Secretary of State for India and also his famous Despatch on the Indian Councils Bill, 1909, will be read with immense interest. Every effort has been made to include in this edition not only all the speeches of Lord Morley on Indian subjects but also his contributions to the press on the same. To facilitate easy reference an index has been added to this edition.

July 1917.

PREFACE.

Advantage has been taken of the issue of this revised (Third) edition to include Lord Morley's views on the Montagu Reforms as well as King Edward's Gracious Proclamation (Appendix F.) which is well known as the handiwork of Lord Morley, the then Secretary of State for India.

MADRAS, The Publishers.
June 1920.

CONTENTS.

APPENDIX.

MORLEY'S INDIAN SPEECHES

INDIAN BUDGET SPEECH FOR 1906

[*The following Speech was delivered by John Morley in the House of Commons in August 1906 in introducing the Indian Budget for the year* :—]

PARLIAMENT'S RESPONSIBILITY TO INDIA.

This is a new Parliament, and I believe it has a long life before it. There are abundant signs that this new Parliament recognises to the full its highest responsibilities for the Government of India. There is on the paper a tolerable scheme of amendments and I, for one, do not make any complaint whatever of it, although it is not altogether convenient from a personal point of view. When we consider all the questions that are involved in Indian policy, all the questions that are associated with this country as well as with India, affecting not merely 300,000,000 people for whom we in this House are the trustees, but also affecting and going to the roots of the strength and stability of this Government and country, I think no one will deny that India holds one of the three or four master-keys of the strength of Britain.

There are some people to whom Indian policy means the North-West Frontier, some to whom it means Persia, others to whom it means opium. *(Hear, hear, and laughter.)* But our Indian policy, when you come to look at it with responsibility, demands a far more comprehensive survey than this, and a due sense of proportion. Of course, it is the tendency of every Minister to exaggerate the importance of his own office. But it is not in the least because I exaggerate the importance of my office that I do believe—I have believed long before I had anything to do with the Government of India—that of all the subjects which engage our attention—for example, in this Session, education, taxation, foreign relations, the Army, the Fleet, North Africa, and South Africa—not one of them exceeds in moment and importance to this country, the wisdom or unwisdom of the policy to be pursued in India. *(Hear, hear.)* What portion of the great realm of Government raises more important issues than India? I am not speaking of the picturesque or the speculative points of view; I am looking at, and I invite this new Parliament to look at, the practical points involved in the Indian case. There is the land frontier on the north-west that involves complex and intractable elements. I would invite the House in passing to notice the great, the enormous transformation of our foreign policy that has taken place since the days of Mr. Canning, Lord Palmerston and Lord Castlereagh. We are no longer concerned in dynastic quarrels in Europe, nor even territorial division in

Europe. Whether it is for good or for ill, whether we like it or not, we see the transformation of our policy into an Asiatic policy. (Mr. Keir Hardie dissented.) My honourable friend does not like that statement; I do not know that I do, but there is the change. The most engrossing and perplexing questions now are those which involve us with China, Japan, Russia, the great Power in Central Asia. These are the questions which now deserve and engross the attention of Parliament and of Ministers. And here I hope my friends who ought to be opposite—(*laughter*)—will allow me an observation. I thought at the time we took a very bad, false step three or four years ago in South Africa. That false step has landed us in inextricable confusion—(*hear, hear*)—that is bad enough. But a really false step taken in India would land us in confusion more dire and disastrous still. The interest of Great Britain in Indian questions is supposed to be languid, and the benches opposite of an Imperial party do not show interest in far the greatest of all Imperial questions. (Mr. John Ward: "There are only six of them," and *cheers.*) Their interest may be languid—(*laughter*)—but, after all, I like to be indulgent. I do not believe that, in the country among those who think about our political position at all, the interest is languid. But even if it were, there are some pretty obvious reasons for it. The subject is very intricate, the terms are unfamiliar, the whole field is vast, distant, and, even to us who are concerned with it, very dim. And this subject kindles none of the fire of party which, as we all know, is the most attractive element in securing crowded benches and long speeches. Still, when people say that India has always been excluded from the sphere of party, I do not believe that. Is it all historically true? After all, when we turn to the old debates under Mr. Pitt and Mr. Fox, and even if we come down to 1880, when Mr. Gladstone won his great and triumphant election, somewhat similar to an election that has followed it, we find some of the very hardest fights in our party history have been fights on Indian questions. I am glad, however, to think that at this moment India is not in any sense or degree a party question. I believe that between myself and the noble Lord opposite, who has had India Office experience, there is only a moderate degree of difference.

PLACING THE SALARY OF THE SECRETARY OF STATE UPON THE ESTIMATES.

My friend, Mr. Keir Hardie, has put on the paper a motion, not unfamiliar, for placing the salary of the Secretary of State upon the Estimates, so that there might be an opportunity, as there is in Irish or Scottish policy, of indulging in criticism and, if possible, of discomfiting the Secretary of State. I have considered all the arguments pretty carefully, and heard many debates in this House on that proposition, and I submit this to the House if he divides on the motion. We are all agreed it is best and wisest to exclude India from the field of our ordinary party operations. (*Cheers.*) See, then, what the carrying of the proposal would mean. On a debate on the Secretary of State's salary, some member very likely would move a reduction, and he would, I am sure, make a considerable number of reasonable criticisms. But does he not see that, when it came to a division, it could not but be a party vote? All the supporters of the Ministry, or nearly all, would go into the lobby to give the Secretary of State his salary, and gentlemen opposite very likely might, in spite of their desire to keep India out of party politics, support the reduction of salary. I cannot think that would do any good. In subjecting details of Indian administration to the supervision and criticism of this House, the Indian Government would be exposed to the kind of criticism which would do no good, but harm. As I say, this proposal has often been discussed in this House before. I think Lord George Hamilton spoke in this sense in resisting a similar motion, as, I am sorry to say, I must resist this motion to-day. You might, as you used to do in old Parliaments, every twenty years appoint a Committee or Commission to travel over the whole field of Indian Government and report upon it. My objection to that would be that it is absurd to bring home all the capable men, who are engaged in the day-to-day administration of the enormous Government, in order to answer questions which would not in all cases be dictated by knowledge, but partly by prejudice and passion. I should be sorry to see that. But I think it would be of the greatest advantage that there should be discussions from time to time on particular questions, either taken out of supply, or perhaps a lenient Government with plenty of time might give time. For example, I think three or four hours might well be spent in this House in discussing education. I have some views of my own about education, and I should very well like to have this House decide the issues that that question opens. Then there is an enormous question in which Radicals in old days used to be deeply interested, and I see no reason why those Radicals should not be interested in it, namely, the partition of the expenditure and cost of military operations between India and England. I have a very shrewd suspicion that that partition of charge is not in all respects equitable. (*Hear, hear.*)

AN ENCOURAGING REVENUE STATEMENT.

I am afraid I must now take the House through a series of figures. I will make them as short as I can. This I ask the House to believe, that in these figures are the real issues; and if you at all realise your responsibility, you must not grudge the intervention of these rather harassing—and, many of them, rather tiresome figures—though not to me. In reciting these figures to the House, I hope it will not be thought that I am holding a brief. To say that I am not indebted to the capable and helpful gentlemen in my office, and in India also, would be the highest ingratitude on my part. But I view these things with an impartial and independent eye and, therefore, I hope the House will not listen to my figures as if they were listening to a lawyer reading a brief. (*Hear, hear, and laughter.*) When I look at the string of amendments on the paper, I cannot but think that they mean, if they mean anything, that the Government of India by this country is a dead failure. (Mr. Lupton, *Hear, hear.*) I do not believe a word of it. (*Loud cheers.*) I do not say that it is incapable of improvement. Like everything else in this world—even the procedure of the House I am addressing—(*laughter*)—it is capable of improvement. But the figures, I am going to recite to the House, are cheerful and encouraging. (*Cheers.*) The net revenue of India in 1904-5 was £49,000,000—I leave out the thousands—the expenditure was £46,000,000, and the surplus was £3,400,000. In 1905-6, the revenue was £48,500,000; the expenditure, £46,750,000; and the surplus, £1,800,000. I now come to the figures of the current year, which, of course, are estimates only:—Revenue, £48,800,000; expenditure, £48,000,000 surplus, £800,000. For some years before 1901-02, the revenue was exposed to certain conditions, with which I need not weary the House; but since then, owing to various causes—the absence of any widespread famine principally—the surpluses have been enlarged.

THE SALT TAX.

What can we do with the surplus? We can remit taxation. I begin with the remission of the tax which

I regard as of great importance—the salt duty. (*Cheers.*) The salt duty has been reduced since 1903-4 by two steps, at a cost of £2,000,000 to the revenue. Rates have been reduced £690,000, and income-tax £200,000. In 1903, Sir Henry Fowler, then not in office, made a very powerful appeal in favour of the remission of the salt duty. That remission has been made. But for my part, I cannot regard, and I will not regard, with satisfaction, or even with patience, the continuance at a high scale of a tax on a prime necessity of life. (*Cheers.*) It is a question, however, that you cannot settle right off, or by a stroke of the pen. But any one who reads the report in the Blue-Book published this year will see that the last remission of the tax, which was considerable, has had a most admirable effect in cheapening the retail price; and the knowledge that they were entitled to the reduction has become known to the most ignorant class in the country. Even the Bheel woman who buys salt by the ounce knows that she is entitled to more than she used to get. What was formerly purchased to last three or four days now lasts five or six days. More salt is also given to cattle. In some provinces the consumption has risen 10 per cent. in the last three years, and the saving per head of the population is reckoned as one day's wages to the poorest of the working classes. (*Cheers.*) I have some figures as to the comparative effect of the imposition of the salt tax in India, and in a famous European country where the tax is still imposed—namely, Italy—but they can wait for another occasion. It is not that the Indian is more heavily burdened in the matter of the salt duty than the Italian. But, however that may be, I am glad to think that the very able and expert financial member of the Viceroy's Council hopes to make a further reduction in the duty, even though he cannot go so far as I should like to go, and sweep the thing away altogether. (*Cheers.*) Let us, therefore, be content to take the half loaf, for it is better than no bread. I should like the House fully to realise the significance of this financial statement. The rise in the national income, of which I have spoken, is automatic, and is derived, I am glad to think, from the taxpayers for value received, Here are significant figures. The land revenue has gone up by £1,500,000, because the productive value of the land has gone up and more land is brought under cultivation. The excise has increased by £1,500,000—partly due, no doubt, to higher duties; but due also to increased consumption. We have all become political economists since the raising of the question of fiscal reform. (*Laughter.*) We, therefore, know that this rise in consumption must be due to increased purchasing power and consequently to greater wage-earning. Customs have risen more than half a million sterling. They are levied in India for revenue purposes only. (*Cheers.*) Why have they risen? Because more manufactured goods of all kinds, especially cotton goods, have been bought, and because more rice, on which there is an export duty, has been exported.

STATE RAILWAYS, IRRIGATION, AND FORESTS.

Still, the most important tributary of the stream so copiously fed from so many affluents is the State railways. I make a present of that to my socialist friends opposite. (Labour *laughter and cheers.*) In India, the State undertakes not only railways, but other gigantic operations for the direct development of the economic resources of the country. It constructs railways and canals; it conducts irrigation operations, it conserves forests. The net revenue under the three heads of railways, canals and forests five years ago was only £2,750,000. What is it to-day? £5,000,000. Therefore, there is a large net increase from these socialistic operations. (Labour *cheers.*) The Indian railway system is really worth thinking about for a moment. It is nearly 30,000 miles in extent, and is growing at the rate of 1,000 miles a year. In the United Kingdom the railway system is 22,634 miles in extent; in Russia it is 40,500 miles, and in the United States 212,000 miles. Of course, we must also look at the areas of the countries concerned. The area of India is 1,000,000 square miles, while the area of Russia is 8½ million square miles, while the area of the United States is 3½ million square miles. These are striking figures, and show that the mileage of India is a good mileage. But let me quote a few more figures about passengers and merchandise, which ought to make the mouths of passengers and merchants here water. In India, in 1905, there were 250,000,000 of passengers and 56,000,000 tons of goods. The average charge for each passenger was one-fifth of a penny per mile, and the average charge for goods was a half penny per ton. (*Cheers.*) Railway directors and governing bodies in this country may well consider whether they cannot bring about a reduction in their railway rates and charges to these low amounts. (*Cheers and laughter.*) The loss which formerly existed on the State railways had fallen gradually, until in 1899-1900 it turned to a modest gain of £70,000, and this has steadily mounted until 1904-05, when it topped £2,000,000. The figures for 1905-06 show a slight fall, but still it topped £1,000,000. The economic effects of this great beneficent action must be pretty obvious to everyone in the House, as, for example, in connexion with the transportation of produce to districts afflicted with scarcity and famine from districts which are more prosperous, in connexion with the inland migration, which is of peculiar importance in India, where some districts are very poor and others worse than poor, and also in connexion with the rapid and satisfactory increase in commerce, which would have been impossible but for this development of railway communication. I am endeavouring to show that India is not an inert and lifeless bureaucracy of official machinery, but a great vital scheme of government. I do not say that government has not its defects; of them the House will hear for the rest of the day. (*Laughter.*) But I wish I had time to dwell on the achievements demanding such skill in engineering, such thought and prudence, such energy in day-to-day administration. (*Hear, hear.*) Some of the amendments on the paper, I think, do less than justice to the vigour with which the great Public Works of India have been prosecuted, increasing the productivity of the ordinary land, protecting acres specially liable to famine, and bringing waste lands into cultivation. I will only mention that the capital expenditure on the large canals up to the end of 1906-07 was 28 millions, yielding a revenue of 7¾ per cent. This year 1¼ million is provided for maintenance and construction, in addition to other sums for minor works. The State forests in India cover an area of 250,000 square miles, and 66,000,000 cubic feet of timber from the State forests have been extracted, and there has been an increase in the forest revenues in five years of more than £600,000. (*Cheers.*) I cannot wonder that those who are concerned in these operations look forward with nothing short of exultation to the day, when this country will realise what a splendid asset is now being built up in India in connexion with these forests. India, whatever gloom famine and plague may spread over her landscape, is at least happy in her immunity from a great burden of national debt—that horrid, spectral figure. The total permanent debt of India, on March 31, 1905, was £214,000,000. This is a pretty large figure, no doubt. But of this, no less than £154,000,000 is represented in railways and irrigation works, leaving only £60,000,000 of ordinary debt. (*Cheers.*) The net charge this year for interest other than interest on railways and irrigation works is £800,000, so that you have the important fact that the railways and irrigation, after meeting all charges for working and interest, yielded a revenue of £3,102,000. That is to say, these receipts cover the interest on the ordinary debt about four times over. (*Cheers.*) That is a very striking and remarkable fact.

EXPORTS AND IMPORTS.

I should now like to pass from these figures to trade. As we all know, a controversy raged in this country some little time ago as to whether exports or imports are the more trustworthy signs of national prosperity. Happily, in India, it does not matter a pin whether you take exports or imports as a test of national prosperity. Ten years ago the value of Indian merchandise and produce exported was £73,000,000; last year it was £105,500,000, or an increase of 44½ per cent. Ten years ago the value of imported merchandise into India was £46,250,000; last year it was £68,750,000, or an increase of 48½ per cent. The value of the gold and silver held in India outside the currency has increased by £9,000,000 a year for five years. There are those who can, with perfect good faith in their own minds, paint the condition of the population of India in lamentable colours, just as you could do in this country. The distribution of material prosperity over this vast continent is unequal. You must remember also that the standard is low. Remember that India is essentially agricultural, with varying degrees of fertility. Pessimist or optimist may make out an equally good case, if they do not go into particular parts of India. There are districts which are poor and unprogressive, like the arid regions of the Deccan. On the other hand, if we go to Bengal, Burma and the newly irrigated portions of the Punjab, we shall find a much more satisfactory state of things. That India is a poor country I do not deny; that the system of government is costly I know; that it is extravagant I suspect. (*A laugh.*) But there is not one of these things I could not say of my own country. (*Cheers.*) We on this side constitute a majority who say that our system of government is costly—I should think it is—(*Hear, hear*) and that it is in some respects extravagant. That is what many of us are here to say. But let us mark the signs of improvement among the diverse populations of India. An experienced native officer, in the course of a review of his work in Sind, speaks of the possession in greater quantity among the people in the villages of articles of copper and brass, finer garments, and silver and gold as well as of houses being built of brick and tiles in place of mud; and what has been said by this native officer of Sind has also been said by native observers in other states. Then you find among the natives such a new-fangled invention as the sewing machine, a machine for crushing the sugarcane instead of the old rude stone implement and the growing use of mineral oil. Some of us may wish the old indigenous handicrafts of the country had remained where they were, and sometimes I am not sure whether I do not belong to that retrograde class. But we cannot go back. India cannot continue to confine herself to those handicrafts. One sign of the change has been the growth of the cotton factories—a sign which is perhaps to the dissatisfaction of some of my friends from Lancashire. From the report of the Chief Inspector of Factories, I find that it has been a year of extraordinary prosperity, but that does not at all prevent my adhesion to a promise which I mentioned to a deputation to despatch an English Factory Inspector to see how the factory rules, such as we have in England, are observed in the different social conditions of India.

INDIA AND FREE TRADE.

The House will now permit me to say a few words on India's relations to Free Trade. Lord George Hamilton, after he had ceased to be Secretary of State, was one of the most powerful exponents, from the Indian point of view, of the impossibility of setting up preferential arrangements. (*Cheers.*) There was also, I think, laid before Parliament an important and well-weighed despatch from Lord Curzon. I think the House will allow me, when I mention the name of that distinguished man, to say that I cannot fail to remember that nobody has ever been more conspicuous or passionate in his self-sacrificing devotion to the interests of India than Lord Curzon. (*Cheers*).

I think the House will desire also that I should express our sympathy with him in the cruel blow that has made his hearth desolate, and that our deepest sympathy with him at this time may help him to bear his stroke with fortitude. (*Hear, hear.*) I do not, however, labour the question of Free Trade, because really the Indian case in this great controversy lies in a nutshell. The strength of India, the prosperity and comfort of India, her trade and commerce, hang on exports. If the market for her food-stuffs and raw materials, her grain, timber, tea and coffee, her supplies of oils, is not ample in volume and favourable in its circumstances, how is she to bear the weight of her expenditure? How does she stand? In 1905-06, the export trade, including Government stores, was £105,000,000; her imports were £69,000,000. But here is the cardinal fact. I am thinking of preferential and discriminating tariffs in favour of the United Kingdom. Of the £105,000,000, the United Kingdom only took 25 per cent. Where did the other portion go? The chief customers for the three-fourths of the exports were the States of Europe, the Far East and the countries bordering on the Indian Ocean.

EARL PERCY:—Can the right honourable gentleman give us the relative proportions of exports from India to the Free Trade States of the Far East, as compared with the Protective States of Europe?

MR. MORLEY:—I am not sure that I can, off-hand. Perhaps, I may be able to give the information later in the afternoon; but it cannot affect this point, whatever may be the answer to the noble Lord's question. This preferential and discriminating policy carries with it that, if India is asked to retaliate and to introduce a preference in our favour, you are asking her to discriminate against three-fourths of her customers in order to satisfy one-fourth. (*Cheers.*) I think that is the case in a nutshell. I will give an illustration from a Foreign Office report on German trade in 1905. It is stated there that in the last four years Germany's bill for Indian produce has risen from £6,000,000 to £10,000,000 per annum, and that the value of German goods sold to India has only risen from £2,000,000 to £2,500,000. What conclusion is to be drawn from that? There are three conclusions to be drawn. First, that the industrial development of Germany does India, at all events, no harm, but good, by widening the market for the raw produce that India has to sell. (*Cheers.*) The second conclusion carries with it the question, "Who gains from this purchasing power of India?" Why, England, because the Indian imports are from the United Kingdom. (*Cheers.*) Lastly, how could it be India's interest to injure a good customer like Germany by a discriminating tariff in favour of English goods?

THE MILITARY SHADOW.

So far, I have given a rose-coloured—I hope a true-coloured—picture. In military expenditure, however, we have the shadow. Comparing broadly 1906-7 with the figures of ten years ago, there is an increase in the strength of the Army of 4,147 men.

In 1896-97, the increase was 227,000 men and in 1906-7, 231,500 men. But the remarkable circumstance comes out that in British cavalry and infantry there is no increase. The only important additions to the fighting strength of the Army are an increase in our artillery and an increase in the number of British officers to the tune of 1,000. That is a large and costly addition, but I will not argue it now. The net Army expenditure in India, British and Native, in 1896-97 was £15,000,000, the estimate for 1906-7 is £18,700,000—an increase of £3,700,000. This has to be divided into two equal items of £1,850,000 for ordinary and special military expenditure. I invite the House to attend to one element in the increase in the ordinary expenditure. The House will remember that the late Government found it necessary to grant additional pay to the non-commissioned officers and men in the British Army in India. Those were circumstances for which neither the Government nor the governed in India had a shadow of responsibility. They were not responsible for those social circumstances which made it necessary to add to the pay of the British soldier, but the increase of pay in the British contingent of the Indian military force was saddled on India to the tune of nearly a million sterling.

LORD KITCHENER'S SCHEME.

I now go for a moment to the special military expenditure associated with the name of Lord Kitchener. From all the information that reaches me, His

Majesty's Government have every reason to be satisfied with the prudence of the decision in the vexed and turbid question of Army organisation made to the Government of India, in my despatch of February or March last. (*Hear, hear.*) I have carefully watched these operations, and I have obtained whatever information I could get on the subject; and I say that in my opinion we have every reason to be satisfied with the decision we then took. I do not discuss Lord Kitchener's scheme and the expense as a whole. In the present stage it is not ripe for discussion, but I will only say that I am engaged in active correspondence with the Government of India upon the various questions involved in this special military expenditure in Lord Kitchener's scheme, and until that correspondence, which also involves some decisions to be taken by the Imperial Defence Committee, is matured, I do not think I can say anything at this stage that would be very profitable for the House to listen to. I will only say, in anticipation of some discussion that is likely to take place this afternoon, that after all you should be fair even to soldiers and generals. (*Laughter.*) You must look at these things as they were presented. This is not a scheme for increasing the Army; only two additional units are sanctioned. The argument in justification of the outlay which my honourable friend behind me (Sir Henry Cotton) will have to meet is that, if the scheme had not been adopted, India would have continued to spend £17,000,000 a year on an Army provided with second rate guns, with too few officers, with bad transport, with defective medical organisation, inadequate reserves and stores. It is said that by paying this £2,000,000 extra for five years and £1,500,000 for recurrent charges for a certain number of years, you will have avoided all the mischief and shortcomings which I have described. That is the military defence. Behind that there lies, no doubt, a large number of disputable facts, inferences and conclusions. In indicating this controversy, I am not going to pledge myself to any line, as far as the present Budget is concerned. I hope the House will not think that it is arrogant on my part. On the contrary, it is modesty. I am not going into this complex and dangerous question, without making perfectly sure that I have all the information to which I can possibly get access, and that I have listened to all the arguments which can be brought against the views I am personally inclined to take. (*Hear, hear.*)

THE "INSOLUBLE PROBLEM."

I am drawing to an end; but I am not sure that the end is not the most important part of what I have to say. I have heard a thousand times that India is an insoluble problem. Well, the man who runs away from problems called "insoluble" is not fit for politics. (*Cheers.*) I have generally found that what is called an insoluble problem is after all a problem wrongly stated. Here we have a new Parliament. I respectfully invite the new Parliament of to-day to look at the India of to-day with a clear, firm and steadfast gaze. I have only been in office a very few months, but I will say of myself—and I hope it will not seem egotistic—that I have lost no opportunity of placing myself in contact with as many people as possible from India, people of every type, of every class, likely to take every different point of view. I have seen native rulers from India—"dusky faces, in white silken turban wreathed"—and I sometimes think we make a mistake in not attaching the weight we ought to, to these powerful princes, as standing forces in India. (Cheers.) Then it has been my business to hear all I could learn from those military officers who keep watch and ward along our frontier among the fierce border tribes. I have seen what is called the "sun-dried bureaucrat"—(*laughter*)—and I have found that what is meant by that phrase is a man eminent for experience, for knowledge and for responsibility, faithfully and honourably discharged. (*Cheers.*) I have seen soldiers, travellers and journalists, and I have kept up a continuous and most useful and interesting correspondence with the Viceroy. Again, I hope the House will not think it egotistic, but I want them to know why I have any right to take any view at all, as to the situation in India. If I were to say that on the strength of these conversations, many and long, I pretend to know all about India, I should be foolish. I do not dogmatise. The man who dogmatises at all is not, I suspect, the wisest of men. But the man who dogmatises about India—and I throw this out for this afternoon's discussion—is a pure simpleton. (*Laughter and cheers.*) I throw that out promiscuously.

(*Laughter.*) I have done my best to read the signs of to-day in India, and it is for the India of to-day that the Government and this House are responsible. I do not believe for a moment that, because you have a comparatively new Viceroy and new Secretary of State, this is enough to make a crisis in this vast dominion.

THE NEW SPIRIT.

What I seem to discern are not at all the symptoms of crisis. I do not see or hear demands for violent or startling new departures. What I do see is a stage reached in the gradual and inevitable working out of Indian policy, which makes it wise and in the natural order of things—and I do not at all despair of securing the agreement of the noble Lord opposite to this—that we should advance with a firm, courageous and intrepid step some paces further on the path of continuous, rational improvement in the Indian system of government. (*Hear, hear.*) Every one—soldiers, travellers and journalists—they all tell us that there is a new spirit abroad in India. Be it so. How could you expect anything else ? You have now been educating the peoples for years with Western ideas and literature. You have already given them facilities for communication with one another. How could you suppose that India could go on just as it was when there was little higher education, and when the contact between one part and another was difficult and infrequent ? How could you think that all would go on as before ? As for education, let the House think of this little fact. There is this year a Senior Wrangler from India; and

I am told by the Master of Trinity that he was Senior wrangler after two years' residence, when all the others in the class had had three years' residence. I mention that, as showing that you cannot go on narrowly on the old lines. We should be untrue to all the traditions of this Parliament, and to those who from time to time and from generation to generation have been the leaders of the Liberal party, if we were to show ourselves afraid of facing and recognising the new spirit with candour and consideration.

THE CONGRESS AND "DISAFFECTION."

I said something about the Indian Princes. It is a question whether we do not persist in holding these powerful men too lightly. Then there is the Congress. I do not say that I agree with all that the Congress desires; but, speaking broadly of what I conceive to be at the bottom of the Congress, I do not see why any one who takes a cool and steady view of Indian Government should be frightened. (*Cheers.*) I will not at once conclude that, because a man is dissatisfied and disconteded, therefore he is disaffected. (*Cheers.*) Why, our own reforms and changes have been achieved by dissatisfied men who were no more disaffected than you or I. If there be disaffection —and there may be some—I will not, as far as I have anything to do with the Government of India, play the game of disaffection by exaggerating the danger or by over-readiness to scent evil. There have been two books recently written about India by gentlemen who accompanied the

Prince of Wales, which I would respectfully recommend honourable members to read. One of these books is by Mr. Abbott, and the other by a gentleman, Mr. Sydney Low, of proved competence in political subjects. Mr. Low is a man who knows what he is writing about, and he says :—

> The journey of the Prince of Wales showed clearly that there is a deep and widespread attachment to the Imperial House among the Indian people ; and even where there is discontent with a mode of Government, there is no feeling against the Throne. Calcutta, when the Prince of Wales visited it, was in the trough of a furious agitation against the Partition of Bengal —an agitation, which on one occasion had caused every native shop to be closed. Yet, when the Prince appeared amongst that angry populace, he was received not only with cordiality, but even with demonstrative enthusiasm.

"SUN-DRIED BUREAUCRATS" AND "PESTILENT AGITATORS."

I am not going, and I hope the House is not going, to be easily frightened when it finds such a state of things together with other facts which are no doubt disagreeable. But that is what politics are. There is a constant ebb and flow of feeling in the countries where there is any political life, and this shows that political life is stirring in India. I deprecate this bandying between different schools of Indian opinion of charges and epithets. One says, "Sun-dried bureaucrats," and the other says, " Pestilent agitators." But the duty of the Secretary of State and of the House of Commons is to rise well above that sort of thing. An observation—a just and salutary observation—has been made that we should adopt, not mawkish or maudlin sentimentality,—(*Laughter.*)

—but a manly desire to understand and comprehend those over whom, for good or evil, we have undertaken to govern. (*Hear, hear.*) We have not ourselves to blame for the great division that separates the European from the native Indian. But there is a root of statesmanship as well as of humanity, contained in the lines, "Hath not a Jew eyes? Hath not a Jew hands, organs, dimensions, affections and passions?" (*Cheers.*) That is what I should like to make the foundation of the education of our competition-wallahs. It was well said once that "great thoughts come from the heart"—a beautiful expression, but I should like to add to it a little prosaic rider of my own—great thoughts come from the heart, but they must go round by the head. (*Cheers.*)

COMING TO CLOSE QUARTERS.

And now I come to close quarters. In all that I have said, I shall not be taken to indicate for a moment that I dream you can transplant British institutions wholesale into India. That is a fantastic and ludicrous dream. (*Opposition cheers.*) Even if it could be done, it would not be for the good of India. You have got to adapt your institutions to the conditions of the country where you are planting them. You cannot transplant bodily the venerable oak of our constitution to India, but you can transplant the spirit of our institutions—the spirit, the temper, the principle and the maxim of British institutions. (*Cheers.*) All these, you can transplant and act upon and abide by. You cannot give universal suffrage in India, and I do not insist that India should be on the same footing as our Self-Governing Colonies like Canada. In the debate on the Indian Council Act in 1892 in this House, Mr. Gladstone said:—"In all these proposals for improved government of India, the Government of India must have the carrying out of those proposals." That is what he said, and I believe more and more, from my own experience, that that is a proved view. I rejoice, and I believe the House will rejoice, that I am authorised to announce on my full responsibility that the Government of India is in thorough sympathy with the necessities of the day and of the hour. I only want the House to know that we are in earnest in the direction that I have indicated. I hope there will be no hurry or precipitancy, either on the part of the bureaucrats or of the agitators. If there is, it can only have the effect, the inevitable effect, of setting the clock back. (*Hear, hear.*)

AN INSTALMENT OF THREE REFORMS.

The very limited amount of time given to the discussion of the Budget in Calcutta has hitherto been rather a scandal. Then there is also the question of the moving of amendments to the proposals of the Viceroy and his advisers. Then there is the extension of the representative element in the Legislative Council—not the Executive Council, but the Legislative. There are three points bearing closely upon our discussion to-day, and I am glad to say that the Governor-General is about to appoint a small committee from his Executive Council to consider what reforms in this direction can be expediently carried forward. I have every reason to believe that I shall, before the end of the Session, have a despatch from the Government of India empowering me to state to this House the definite results at which the Governor-General and his committee have arrived.

EMPLOYMENT OF INDIANS IN THE HIGHER OFFICES.

In regard to the question of the employment of Indians in the higher offices, I think a move—a definite and deliberate move—ought to be made, with the view of giving competent and able natives the same access to the higher posts in the administration that are given to our own countrymen. (*Cheers.*) There is a famous sentence in the Queen's Proclamation of 1858 which says:—

> It is our further will that, so far as may be, our subjects, of whatever race or creed, be freely and impartially admitted to offices in our service, offices the duties of which they may be qualified by their educational talents and ability duly to discharge.

I think those words, "so far as may be," have been somewhat misinterpreted in the past. I do not believe that the Ministers who advised Queen Victoria in framing one of the most memorable documents in all our history meant those words to be construed in a narrow, literal, restricted or pettifogging sense. (*Cheers.*) I do not believe that Parliament ever intended this promise of the Queen's should be construed in any but a liberal and generous sense. The Governor-General of India to-day is, I am glad to say, a man of a firm texture of mind. I do not believe the Governor-General has any intention of riding off on a narrow interpretation of a promise which was as wise and politic, as it was just. (*Hear, hear.*)

THE CHARACTER OF THE GOVERNMENT IN INDIA.

I do not know if there is any case in history of an autocratic, personal or absolute Government co-existing with free speech and free right of meeting. For as long a time as my poor immagination can pierce through, for so long a time our Government in India must partake, and in no small degree, of the personal and absolute element. But that is no reason why we should not try this great experiment of showing that you can have a strong and effective administration along with free speech and free institutions, and being all the better and all the more effective because of free speech and free institutions. (*Cheers.*) That policy is a noble one to think of, but the task is arduous; and because it is noble and because it is arduous, I recommend the policy, of which I have only given a broad outline, to the adoption of the House. (*Cheers.*)

INDIAN BUDGET SPEECH FOR 1907

[*The following speech was delivered by Mr. Morley in the House of Commons on June* 6, 1907 *in introducing the Budget for the year* :—]

I am afraid I shall have to ask the House for rather a large draft upon its indulgence. The Indian Secretary is like the aloe, which, I think, blooms once in a hundred years, for he only troubles the House with speeches of his own, once in twelve months.

THE BRITISH DEMOCRACY AND INDIA.

There are several topics which the House will expect me to say something about, and there are two or three topics of supreme interest and importance for which I will plead for the patient and comprehensive consideration of the House. We are too apt to find that gentlemen here and outside fix upon an incident of which they read in the newspaper; they put it under a microscope, and then indulge in reflections upon it, and they regard that as taking an intelligent interest in the affairs of India. If we could suppose that on some occasion within the last three or four weeks a wrong turn had been taken in judgment in Simla, or in the Cabinet, or in the India Office, or that to-day in this House some wrong turn might be taken, what disasters would follow, what titanic efforts to repair these disasters, what devouring waste of national and Indian treasure lost, and what a wreckage would follow in the train! I submit that these are quite certain or possible consequences which misjudgment either here or in India, or among His Majesty's Government, might bring with it. I believe I am not going too far when I say that this is almost, if not quite, the first occasion upon which what is called the British democracy in its full strength has been brought directly face to face with the difficulties of Indian Government, with all their intricacies, all their complexities, and, above all, all their subtleties, and their enormous magnitude. Last year, when I had the honour of addressing the House on the Indian Budget, I observed, as others have done before me, that it was one of the most difficult experiments that had ever been tried in human history, whether you can carry on—I think for myself you will have to carry on in India—personal government along with free speech and free right of public meeting. That which last year was partially a speculative question has this year become more or less actual. I want to set out the case as frankly as I possibly can. I want, if I may say so without persumption, to take the House into full confidence, so far—and let nobody quarrel with this provision—as public interest will allow. I will ask the House to remember that we do not only hear one another; we are ourselves this afternoon overheard. Words that may be spoken here are overheard in the whole kingdom. They are overheard thousands of miles away by a great and complex community—by those who are doing the service and work of the Crown in India, by those who take part in the great work of commercial and non-official life in India, by the great Indian Princes who are outside British India, by the great dim masses of Indians whom, in spite of all, we persist in regarding as our friends, and by those whom, I am afraid, we must reluctantly call our enemies. This is the reason why everybody, who speaks to-day including myself, must use language which is well advised, of reserve, and, as I say again, of comprehensive consideration.

A WORD ON FINANCE.

The subject of discussion being the Indian Budget I must turn for a moment to finance. I assume that all the Members of the House have entirely mastered the statement of the details of the accounts and estimates for the three years 1905—6, 1906—7, and 1907—8. I assume that these are in the mind of every member of this House. Last year I told the House that I could not regard with patience the salt tax—a tax upon a necessary of life. I am glad to be able to say that the salt tax, which was reduced by half a rupee in 1903, and by half a rupee in 1905, has now been reduced in 1907—8. I greatly rejoice because, after all, the rise in the consumption of salt in consequence of this reduction of duty proved that it weighed upon the people. The cost of this reduction is £3,000,000. These reductions amount to 60 per cent. of the tax as it stood before March 1903. After allowing for the effects of the reduction on salt, and the diminution, to be computed, of the revenue from opium of £600,000, we anticipate a surplus of three quarters of a million pounds. All surpluses are satisfactory. This surplus is due to two causes. The first is the agricultural prosperity, and the second is that we have decided, in consultation with the Government of India, to reduce the military expenditure for the year by £500,000. I am glad that that meets with approval. The end of all is, that our financial position is sound and we have a splendid security to offer for all loans that are raised in this country for Indian purposes and on Indian securities.

MILITARY EXPENDITURE.

One other particular, which it is hard to mention without a good deal of controversy, is the great cost of the training of the British troops in India. Payments by India to the War office in respect of the training of British troops for service in India is half a million pounds per annum. The method of calculating this charge has not, I think, been changed for twenty years, and for some time it has been admitted that it should be submitted to investigation. All I can say is that my right hon'ble friend here (Mr. Haldane) will find a dragon in his path towards the Indian gold mine. Meantime, the controversy between us being unsettled, a committe has been appointed with my right hon'ble friend's consent, which will begin work in the autumn, to ascertain the proportion of these charges that should be borne respectively by this country and by India. Lord Justice Romer will, I am glad to say, be the Chairman of that Committee, Lord Welby will be a member of it, and we shall agree upon a third member. There will also be three representatives of the India Office and two representatives of the War Office; and I hope the result of their deliberations will be that some scheme or schedule of the respective charges will be arrived at, which will do justice to the British tax payer and justice also to the Indian tax payer.

EXTENSION OF RAILWAYS.

There is one very important subject which I wish also to press upon the attention of the House—namely, the extension of the railway system. There, again, I am well aware of the enormous interest taken by traders in this country, and the interest taken, or not taken, but which ought to be taken by people living in India, in the extension of the railway enterprise in India. Here, again, I have been fortunate enough to get a Committee of experts to go to India for the purpose of examining carefully into the details of railway administration and how far the complaints are well-founded and justified. So much for railways.

THE SHADOW OF PLAGUE.

The Budget is a prosperity Budget, but I am free to admit that a black shadow falls across the prospect. The plague figures are appalling. But do not let us get unreasonably excited, even about these appalling figures. If we had reviewed the plague figures last September, we might have hoped that this horrible scourge was on the wane. From 920,000 deaths in the year 1900, the figures went up to 1,1000,000 in 1904, and they exceeded 1,000,000 in 1905. In 1906 a gleam of hope arose, and the mortality sank to something under 500,000. The combined efforts of the Government and of the people produced that reduction; but, alas, since January, 1907, the plague has again flared up in districts that had been filled with its terror for a decade. For the first four months of this year the deaths were 642,000, and exceeded the record for the same period in any past year. You must remember that we have to cover a very vast area, and I do not know if these figures would appeal to us if we took the area of the whole of Europe. It was in 1896 that the plague first appeared in India, and up to April, 1907, the total figure of those human beings who have died is 5,250,000. But, dealing with a population of 300 millions, this great mortality, although enormous, is not all comparable with the black death and other scourges which spread over Europe in earlier times, in proportion to the population. The plague mortality, which was higher this year than in 1904, only represents a death-rate of about three per 1,000. It is local and particularly centres in the Punjab, the United Provinces and Bombay. No one, I do not care to what school of Indian thought he belongs, can deny that measures for the extermination and mitigation of this disease have occupied the most serious, constant, unflagging, zealous and energetic attention of the Government of India. But the difficulties we encounter are enormous. It is possible that men may rise this afternoon and say that we are not enforcing with sufficient zeal proper sanitary rules, but I am certain other hon'ble members will get up to show that the great difficulty in the way of sanitary rules being observed arises from the reluctance of the population to practise them. They are naturally suspicious, and when all these new rules are forced upon them they naturally resent and resist them. I will not detain the House with the details of all the proceedings we are taking. We have instituted long scientific inquiries with the aid of the Royal Society of India. There are very intelligent officers, who are doing all they can to trace the roots of this disease, and to discover, if they can, any means to prevent it. It is a curious thing that, while there appears to be no immunity from this frightful scourge for the natives, there is an almost entire immunity for Europeans. It is difficult to understand this immunity.

RIGHTEOUSNESS AND OPIUM REVENUE.

I have reason to believe that an enormous number of gentlemen in this House are greatly interested in opium. Judging by the amount of correspondence I receive on the subject of opium, the interest of all the Churches and of both political parties, and of all the groups is very sincere and very deep. I notice that the resolutions with which they favour me often use the expression, "Righteousness before revenue".

Yes, but you must not satisfy your own righteousness at the expense of other people's revenue.

MR. LUPTON :—We are quite ready to bear the expense of our righteousness.

MR. MORLEY :—I present that observation hopefully to the Chancellor of the Exchequer—no, not very hopefully. This question touches the conscience of the people of this country very deeply. My hon'ble friend sometimes goes a little far; still, he represents a considerable body of feeling. Last May, when the opium question was raised in this House, something fell from me which reached the Chinese Government, and the Chinese Government, on the strength of that utterance of mine made in the name of his Majesty's Government, have persistently done their best to come to some sort of arrangement and understanding with his Majesty's Government upon the subject of opium. In September an Imperial decree was issued in China ordering the strict prohibition of the consumption and cultivation of opium, with a view to the ultimate eradication of all the evils of that evil habit in the space of ten years. A correspondence took place with my right hon'ble friend Sir Edward Grey and since then there has been a considerable correspondence, some of which the House is, by question and answer, acquainted with. The Chinese Government have been always assured, not only by my words spoken in May, but by the Foreign Secretary, that the sympathy of his country was with the objects set forth in their decree of

September. Then a very important incident, as I regard it, and one I think likely to prove very fruitful, was the application by the United States Government to our Government for a joint inquiry into the opium traffic by the United States and the other powers concerned. The House knows, by question and answer, that His Majesty's Government think that procedure by way of commission rather than by way of conference is the right way to approach the question. But no one can doubt for a moment considering the enormous interest the United States have shown on previous occasions, that some good result will come from this.

EARL PERCY :—Will other powers participate in this inquiry besides ourselves?

MR. MORLEY :—Oh yes, certainly. I think that has already been stated to the House by the Foreign Secretary. The point was that the United States Government wished to be informed whether His Majesty's Government were willing to take part in a joint international commission of investigation, and whether certain other powers were likewise willing. I think the noble Lord will find that all the greater powers have been consulted, I will not detain the House with the details, but certainly it is a great satisfaction to know that a great deal of talk as to the Chinese interest in the suppression of opium being fictitious is unreal. I was much struck by a sentence written by the correspondent of the *Times* at Peking recently. Everybody who knows him is aware that he is not a sentimentalist, yet he used remarkable language. He said that he viewed the development in China of the anti-opium movement as encouraging; that the movement was certainly popular, and was supported by the entire Native Press, while a hopeful sign was that the use of opium was fast becoming unfashionable, and would become more so. A correspondence, so far as the Government of India is concerned, is in progress, Those of my hon'ble friends who think we are lacking, perhaps in energy and zeal, I would refer to the language used by Mr. Baker, a very able Finance Member of the Viceroy's Council, because these words really define the position of the Government of India:—

> What the eventual outcome will be it is impossible to foresee. The practical difficulties which China has imposed on herself are enormous, and may prove insuperable, but it is evident that the gradual reduction and eventual extinction of the revenue that India has derived from the trade has been brought a stage nearer, and it is necessary for us to be prepared for whatever may happen.

He added that twenty years ago, or even less, the prospect of losing a revenue of 5½ crores a year would have caused great anxiety, and even now the loss to Indian finances would be serious and might necessitate recourse to increased taxation; but if as they had a clear right to expect, the transition was effected with due regard to finance, and was spread over a term of years, the consequence need not be regarded with apprehension.

THE AMIR'S VISIT.

When I approach military expenditure, and war and the dangers of war, I think I ought to say a word about the visit of the Amir of Afghanistan, which excited so much attention, and kindled so lively an interest in great parts, not only of our own dominions, but in Asia. I am persuaded that we have reason to look back on that visit with the most entire and complete satisfaction. His Majesty's Government, previously to the visit of the Amir, instructed the Governor-General in Council on no account to open any political questions with the Amir. That was really part of the conditions of the Amir's visit; and the result of that policy, which we looking back on it regarded as we did before, has been to place our relations with the Amir—a very important person—on an eminently satisfactory footing, a far better footing than would have been arrived at by any formal premeditated convention. The Amir himself made a speech when he arrived at Cabul on his return, and I am aware that in that speech I come to a question of what may seem a party or personal character, which it is not in the least my intention to deal with. This is what the Amir said on April 10:—

The officers of the Government of India never said a word on political matters; they kept their promise. But as to myself, whenever and wherever I found an opportunity, I spoke indirectly on several matters which concerned the interest of my country and nation. The other side never took undue advantage of it and never discussed with me on those points which I mentioned. His Excellency's invitation (Lord Minto's) to me was in such a proper form that I had no objection to accept it. The invitation which he sent was worded in a quite different form from that on the occasion of the Delhi Durbar. In the circumstances I had determined to undergo all risks (at the time of the Delhi Durbar), and, if necessary, to sacrifice all my possessions and my own life, but not to accept such an invitation as was sent to me for coming to join the Delhi Durbar.

These things are far too serious for me or anybody

to indulge in controversy upon, but it is a satisfaction to be able to point out to the House that the policy we instructed the Governor-General of India in Council to follow has so far worked extremely well.

LORD KITCHENER'S SCHEMES.

I will go back to the army. Last year when I referred to this subject, I told the House that it would be my object to remove any defects that I and those who advise me might to discover in the army system, and more especially, of course, in the schemes of Lord Kitchener. Since then, with the assistance of two very important Committees, well qualified by expert military knowledge, I came to the conclusion that an improved equipment was required. Hon'ble gentlemen may think that my opinion alone would not be worth much ; but after all, civilians have got to decide these questions—and, provided that they arm themselves with the full expert knowledge of military authorities, it is their voice which settles the matter. Certain changes were necessary in the allocation of units in order to enable the troops to be better trained, and therefore our final conclusion was that the special military expenditure shown in the financial pages of the Blue Book must go on for some years more. But the House will see that we have arranged to cut down the rate of the annual grant, and we have taken care —and this, I think, ought to be set down to our credit —that every estimate for every item included in the programme shall be submitted to vigilant scrutiny here as well as in India. I have no prepossession in favour of military expenditure, but the pressure of facts, the pressure of the situation, the possibilities of contingencies that may arise, seem to me to make it impossible for any Government or any Minister to acquiesce in the risks on the Indian frontier. We have to consider not only our position with respect to foreign powers on the Indian frontier, but the turbulent border tribes. All these things make it impossible—I say nothing about internal conditions—for any Government or any Minister with a sense of responsibility to wipe out, or in a high-handed or cavalier way to deal with this military programme.

INHERITED INTERNAL TROUBLES.

Now I come to what I am sure is in the minds of most members of the House—the political and social condition of India. Lord Minto became Viceroy, I think, in November, 1905, and the present Government succeeded to power in the first week of December. Some of the criticisms which I have seen on the attitude of Lord Minto and His Majesty's Government leaves out of account the fact that Lord Minto did not come quite into a haven of serenity and peace. (Mr. Churchill: The monsoon had burst). Yes, very fierce monsoons had broken out on the Olympian heights at Simla, in the camps, and in the Councils at Downing Street. This was the inheritance into which Lord Minto came. It was rather a formidable inheritance, for which I do not, this afternoon, for one moment attempt to distribute the responsibility. It is no affair of mine. Still, when Lord Minto and myself came into power our policy was necessarily, by the conditions under which the case had been left, to compose an unexampled condition of controversy and confusion. In one famous case we happily succeeded, but in Eastern Bengal, for a time, we did not succeed. When I see it declared in articles which always begin with the preamble that the problem of India is altogether outside party questions, I well know from experience that it is the forerunner of a regular Party attack. They say: "Oh there has been supineness on the part of Lord Minto and other persons—supineness, vacillation and hesitation." Sir, there has been no vacillation, no hesitation from December, 1905, up to the present day.

THE FULLER EPISODE.

I must say a single word about one episode, and it is with sincere regret that I refer to it. It is called the Fuller Episode. I have had the pleasure of many conversations with Sir Bampfylde Fuller since his return, and I recognise to the full his abilities, his good faith, and the dignity and self-control with which he, during all this period of controversy, has never for one moment attempted to defend himself or to plunge into any sort of contest with the Viceroy or His Majesty's Government. I think conduct of that kind deserves our fullest recognition. I recognise to the full his gifts and his experience, but I am sure that if he were in this House he would not quarrel with me in saying that those gifts were not well-adapted to the situation which he had to face. Gentlemen opposite may be inclined to take a view hostile to Lord Minto, but I would just remind them that Lord Minto, happily for me, was appointed by their own Government.

MR. BALFOUR :—Why should we be hostile ?

MR. MORLEY :—I do not for a moment suggest that the right hon'ble gentleman is hostile, but I have seen expressions of hostility from his friends. I would not dream of criticising the right hon'ble gentleman or any of his more serious friends. But that position has been taken up. What was the case ? The Lieutenant-Governor suggested a certain course. The Government of India thought it was a mistake, and told him so. The Lieutenant-Governor thereupon said, "Very well, then I am afraid I must resign." There was nothing in all that except what was perfectly honourable to Sir Bampfylde Fuller. But does anybody take up this position that if a Lieutenant-Governor says, "If I cannot have my own way, I will resign," then the Supreme Government of India is bound to refuse to accept that resignation ? All I can say is I do not care who the man may be, but if any gentleman in the Indian service says he will resign unless he can have his own way, then, so far as I am concerned in the matter, his resignation will be accepted. It is said now that Sir Bampfylde Fuller recommended certain measures about education, and that the Government have now adopted them. That is not so. Well, wait. I should like to say that the circumstances are completely changed. What was thought by Lord Minto and the Government of India to be a rash and inexpedient course in those days—the circumstances have changed. I will only mention to the House one point. There was a statement the other day in a very important newspaper that the condition of anti-British feeling in Eastern Bengal had gained in virulence since Sir Bampfylde Fuller's resignation. This, the Viceroy assures me, is an absolute perversion of the facts. The whole atmosphere has changed for the better. When I say that Lord Minto was justified in the course he took, I say it without any prejudice to Sir Bampfylde Fuller, or any prejudice to his future prospects.

THE TROUBLES IN THE PUNJAB.

Now I come to the subject of the disorders. (Several Liberal Members: "Speak up; we cannot hear you.") I am sincerely sorry—because at this point I should like to be heard, if possible, by my hon'ble friends who sit on this side of the House. Disorder has broken out in the Punjab, and I think I may assume that the House is aware of the general circumstances from answers to questions. Under the Regulation of 1818 violent coercive measures were adopted. And I would tell the House frankly, so far as I can—making the reservation that the public interest needs—that it would be quite wrong, in dealing with the unrest in the Punjab, not to mention two circumstances which provided the fuel for the agitation. There were ravages by the plague, and these ravages have been cruel. Again, the seasons have not been favourable. A second cause was that an Act was on the anvil which was believed to be injurious to the condition of a large body of men. Those conditions affecting the Colonisation Act were greatly misrepresented. An Indian member of the Punjab Council pointed out how impolitic he thought it was; but, as I told the House about a week ago, the Viceroy, declining to be frightened by the foolish charge of pandering to agitation, and so forth, refused his assent to that proposal. But in the meantime the proposal of the Colonisation Law had become a weapon in the hands of the preachers of sedition.

I suspect that my hon'ble friend, Sir Henry Cotton, is of opinion that this mischief connected with the Colonisation Act accounted for the disturbance. But I call his attention to this fact, and in order that the House may understand whether or not the Colonisation Act was the main cause of the disturbance. We submit that it was not. There were twenty-eight meetings held by the leading agitators in the Punjab. Of these five only related, even ostensibly, to agricultural grievances; the remaining twenty-three were all purely political. Lala Lajpat Rai took part in two of these meetings, of which one related to the Colonisation Bill and the other was political; and Ajit Singh took part in thirteen, of which only two related to agrarian grievances, and the remaining eleven were political. I hope those who take up the position that this was an agrarian movement and not a political movement in the Punjab will see that the facts are against any such contention. The figures seem to dispose of the contention that agrarian questions are at the root of the present unrest in the Punjab. On the contrary, it rather looks as if there was a deliberate heating of the political atmosphere preparatory to the agrarian meeting at Rawal Pindi on April 21, which gave rise to the troubles.

THE CASE FOR DEPORTATION.

Now what did the Lieutenant-Governor do, and what has he started? He visited twenty-seven out of twenty-nine districts.

SIR HENRY COTTON:—When was that?

MR. MORLEY:—I have not got the date by me. It was in March or April. The Lieutenant-Governor said the situation was different in different parts of the country, that it was serious, and was growing worse, and that the speeches that were being made were directly fomenting sedition. The speeches of Lala Lajpat Rai were very greatly dominated by sedition, and by a good deal of intolerable rhodomontade—and they were published broadcast, even on the floor of this House. The speeches of this agitator, as well as the language used by Ajit Singh, were scattered all over India. These malicious incitements to revolt I will not be an instrument in further disseminating. The Lieutenant-Governor then declared that the situation was urgent and ought not to go on. Sir Denzil Ibbetson described Lajpat Rai thus:—

A revolutionary and a political enthusiast, who had been carried away by his theories into the most intense hatred of the British Government, but that his private character appeared to be above reproach. He has been careful, Sir Denzil adds, "throughout the agitation to keep himself as far as possible in the back-ground, while engineering the systematic propagandism of the last few months."

This is a point to which, I think, the House will attach full importance. The Lieutenant-Governor was satisfied on information obtained practically from all over the Punjab from many diverse sources, of which I am satisfied myself, that Lala Lajpat Rai has been the organiser-in-chief of the agitation and of the systematic propagandism of the last few months in the Province, and that he is "the individual chiefly responsible for the present situation." In this agitation "special attention," it is stated, "has been paid to the Sikhs, and, in the case of Lyallpur, to the military pensioners. Special efforts have been made to secure their attendance at meetings, to enlist their sympathies, and to inflame their passions. So far the active agitation has been virtually confined to the district in which the Sikh element is predominant." The Sikhs, as the House is aware, are the best soldiers in India. "Printed invitations and leaflets," it is added, "have been principally addressed to villages held by Sikhs; and at a public meeting at Ferozepur, at which disaffection was openly preached, the men of the Sikh Regiments stationed there were specially invited to attend," and several hundreds of them, to my amazement, acted upon the invitation. They were told that it was by their aid, and owing to their willingness, in the days of the Mutiny, to shoot down their fellow-countrymen, that the Englishmen retained their hold upon India. And then a particularly vile line of argument was taken. It was asked, "How is it that the plague attacks the Indians and not the Europeans ?" "The Government," said these men, "have mysterious means of spreading the plague; the Government spreads the plague by poisoning the streams and wells." In some villages, in consequence of this representation, the inhabitants actually ceased to use the wells. I was informed only the other day by an officer who is in the Punjab at this moment that, when visiting the settlements, he found the villagers disturbed in mind on this point. He said to his men, "Open up the kits, and see whether these horrible things are in them." The men did as they were ordered, but the suspicion was so great that they insisted upon the glass of the telescope with whose aid the kits were examined being unscrewed, in order to be quite sure that there was no pill behind the glass.

But it may be asked, "Why do you not prosecute them ?" I think Sir Denzil Ibbetson gave a good reason, and for my part I entirely approve of it. It has been found by experience that a prosecution spreads far and wide the matter to which objection is taken. It brings it to the ears of thousands who would never have heard of it otherwise, and it attracts public attention to the prosecution of men who pose as martyrs for the good of their country and people. The speeches of counsel are often almost as harmful as the original matter. Then when the sentences are pronounced, there are pathetic scenes in

Court; there are accounts published of how they are attended on the road to prison. Sometimes the offenders receive the benediction of their leaders, and on release are carried triumphantly through the streets.*

Think of the emergency and the risk! Suppose a single native Regiment had by chance sided with the rioters. A blaze might have been kindled, because accidents in India may lead to dire results. I say it would have been absurd for us, having got a weapon in our hands by law—not an exceptional law, but a standing law—in the face of the risk of a conflagration, it would have been absurd for us not to use that weapon and I for one have no apology whatever to offer for using it. It will be said that it is a dangerous power, I know it. Nobody appreciates more than I do the danger and mischiefs and iniquities in our older history, and perhaps, it may be in present history, of what is called "Reason of State." I know all about that. "Reason of State" is full of mischief and full of danger; but so is sedition, and I should have incurred criminal responsibility if I had opposed the resort to this law. A right honourable gentleman opposite (Mr. Balfour) is in an ironical mood. I will deal with that directly.

THE SITUATION IN EASTERN BENGAL.

I do not wish to detain the House with the story of events in Eastern Bengal and Assam. They are of a different character from those in the Punjab, and in consequence of these disturbances the Government of India, with our approval, have issued an Ordinance, which I am sure the House is familiar with, under the authority and in the terms of an Act of Parliament. The course of events in Eastern Bengal appears to have been mainly this—first, attempts to impose the boycott on Mahomedans by force; secondly, complaints by Hindus that the local officials stop them and by Mahomedans that they do not try to stop them; thirdly, retaliation by Mahomedans; fourthly, complaints by Hindus that the local officials do not protect them from this retaliation; fifthly, general lawlessness of the lower classes on both sides, encouraged by the spectacle of fighting among the higher classes; sixthly, more complaints against the officials as the result of that disorder in certain districts having been complained of. The result of the Ordinance has been that down to May 29 it had not been necessary to take action in any one of these districts.

COERCION IN IRELAND AND INDIA.

I noticed the ironical cheer on the part of the right hon'ble gentleman, the leader of the Opposition, when I referred with perfect freedom to my assent to the resort to weapon we had in the law against sedition, and I have had communications from friends of mine that in this assent I am outraging the principles of a lifetime. I should be ashamed, if I detained the House more than two minutes on anything so small as my life. That can very well take care of itself. But I began this afternoon by saying that this is the first time that British democracy in the full strength, as represented in this House, is face to face with the enormous difficulties of Indian Government. Some of my hon'ble friends, perhaps my right hon'ble friend, look even more in sorrow than in anger upon this alleged backsliding of mine. Last year I told the House that, in my view, India for a long time to come, as far as my imagination could reach, would be the theatre of absolute and personal Government. That, I know, aroused some doubts. Reference has been made to my having resisted the Crimes Act of the right hon'ble gentleman in Ireland. I quite agree that there is apparently a scandalous inconsistency between opposing that policy—it was not a measure so much as a policy—and supporting the deportation of these two men and other men who may follow, if it should be prove to be necessary. But that inconsistency can only be established by taking the position that Ireland is exactly on the same footing as these 300 millions of people—composite, heterogeneous, with different races, and with different faiths. Does anybody contend that any political principle is capable of application in any sort of circumstances and without reference to the conditions? I, at all events, have never taken that view.

I would like to assure my hon'ble friends that in such ideas as I have, about political principles, the leader of my generation was Mr. Mill. There he was, a great and benignant lamp of wisdom and humanity, and I and others kindled our modest rushlights at that lamp. What did Mill say about the Government of India? Remember he was not only that abject being—a philosopher. He spent a large part of his life in active, responsible and experienced concern in the Government of India. If there is anybody who can be quoted as having been the champion of representative government it is Mr. Mill, and his book, I take it, is still the classic book on that subject. And what does he say in the last chapter of that book?

> Government by the dominant country is as legitimate as any other, if it is the one which in the existing state of civilsation of the subject people most facilitates their transition to our state of civilisation.

Then he says this:—

> The ruling country ought to be able to do for its subjects all that could be done by a succession of absolute monarchs guaranteed by irresistible force against the precariousness of tenure, attendant on barbarous despotisms and qualified by their genius to anticipate all that experience has taught to the more advanced nations. If we do not attempt to realise this ideal, we are guilty of a dereliction of the highest moral trust that can devolve upon a nation.

THE BUREAUCRACY SELF CONDEMNED.

I will now ask the attention of the House for a moment while I examine a group of communications from officers of the Indian Government, and if the House will allow me, I will tell them what to my mind is the result of all these communications as to the feeling in India. I mean the general feeling, because that, after all, is what really concerns us. All this unrest in Eastern Bengal and the Punjab will sooner or later—sooner, I hope—pass away. But what is the condition of the mind of India, what is the situation in India in the view of experienced officers at this monent? I ask the House to bear with me when I say that, even now when we are passing through all our stress and anxiety, it is a mistake not to look at the thing rather largely. They all admit that there is a fall in the influence of European officers over the population. They all, or nearly all, admit that there is estrangement—or I ought to say, perhaps, refrigeration—between officers and people. For the last few years—this is a very important point—the doctrine of administrative efficiency has been pressed too hard. The wheels of the huge machine have been driven too fast. Our administration—so shrewd observers and very experienced observers assure me—would be a great deal more popular if it was a trifle less efficient, and a trifle more elastic generally. We ought not to put mechanical efficiency at the head of our ideas. But I am leading up to a particular point. The district officer who represents British rule to the majority of the population is over-worked. He is forced into mere official relations, which are apt to be more disagreeable than agreeable. Experienced judges say that the loose, irregular system of earlier days was better fitted than the regular system of latter days to win and to keep personal influence. Our danger is the creation in the centre of Indian Government of a pure bureaucracy. Competent, honourable, faithful, and industrious, the servants of the State in India are and will be, but if the present system is persisted in, they are likely to become rather mechanical, rather lifeless, perhaps I might even say, rather soul-less. An urgent demand for perfectly efficient administration, I need not tell the House, has a tendency to lead to over-centralisation; it is inevitable. The tendency in India is to override local authority, to force administration to run in official grooves, and so on. The House can imagine the consequences. I would spare no pains to improve our relations with the Native Governments. I would recognise more and more their potential value as a safety valve. I would use my best endeavours to make these States independent in matters of administration. All the evidence tends to show we are rather making administration less personal, and everything also tends to show that the Indian is peculiarly responsive to sympathy. Let us try to draw to our side those men who now influence the people. I believe for my part that most of the people of India are on our side. I do not say for a moment that they like us; but no matter; they know that their whole interest is bound up with the law and order we preserve, and which they know would be shattered to pieces if we disappeared.

A ROYAL COMMISSION AS REMEDY.

But I will come to my point. There is a motion on the paper for an inquiry by means of Parliamentary Committee or Royal Commission into the causes at the root of the dis-satisfaction. Now, I have often thought, while at the India office, whether it would be a good thing to have what they used to have in old days, whenever the East India company's Charter was renewed—a Parliamentary Joint Committe or Commission. I have considered the matter with the greatest attention, and have discussed it with Lord Minto, and I have come to the conclusion that such inquiry would not produce any of the advantages such as were gained in the old days of old Committees, while it would produce a good many drawbacks and would lead to all kinds of difficulties. But I have determined, after consulting with the Viceroy, that considerable advantage might be gained by a Royal Commission to examine, with the experience we have gained over many years, into this great mischief—for everybody knows, all the people in India who have any responsibility know, that it is a great mischief, this over-centralisation. So acute a man of genius as Sir Henry Maine, before he departed, left it as an open question whether Mr. Bright had not been right all along when he said, just before or just after the Mutiny, that the centralised Government of India, such as we have now, was too much for the power of any man to work. Now, when two men, quite unlike in temperament and training, agreed, as to the evil of centralisation on this large scale, it makes one reflect. I will not undertake at the present time to refer to a large Commission, such as was contemplated by Sir H. Maine and Mr. Bright, the large questions of which I have spoken, but I do think much might be gained by an inquiry on the spot into the working of centralisation of Government in India, how in the opinions of trained men here and in India, this mischief might be alleviated. But that is not a question before us now.

EDUCATED INDIA.

You often hear men talk of the educated section of India as mere handful, an infinitesimal fraction. So they are in numbers. But it is idle—fatally idle to say—that this infinitesimal fraction does not count. This educated section makes all the difference, is making and will make all the difference. That the educated section should attack the present system of Government has been long foreseen, has long been known to be inevitable. There need be no surprise in the fact that they want a share of political influence, that they want the emoluments of administration. The means of many of them are scanty, and they think they have little to lose and something to gain by a revolutionary change. But they cannot but know that all their hopes depend on order. They see that the British hand works the State machine surely and smoothly, and they think, having no fear of race animosities, that their hands could work the machine as surely and as smoothly as the British hand. From my observations I should say they could not do it for a week. It is one of the most elaborate systems that ever existed in the history of human Government, and it would break down.

THE REFORMS.

I come now to the last topic—not at all an unimportant one—with which I will trouble the House. Last autumn the Governor-General appointed a Committee of the Executive Council to consider the development of the administrative machinery, and at the end of March last he publicly informed his Executive Council that he had sent home a Despatch to the Secretary of State proposing suggestions for a move in advance. This was not in accordance with instructions from us; it emanated entirely from the Government of India. Now let us consider this. The Viceroy with a liberal—I do not use the word in a party sense—with a liberal, courageous mind entered deliberately upon the path of improvement. The public in India were aware of it. They waited, and are now waiting the result with the liveliest interest and curiosity. Meanwhile, the riots happened in Rawalpindi, in Lahore. After these riots broke out, what was the course we ought to take? Some in this country lean to the opinion—and it is excusable—that the riots ought to suspend all suggestions and talk of reform. Sir, His Majesty's Government considered this view, and in the end they took, very determinedly, the opposite view. They held that such a withdrawal from a line of policy suggested by the Governor-General would, of course, have been construed as a triumph for the party of sedition and of the enemies of the Viceroy. They held that, to draw back on account of local and sporadic disturbances, however serious, anxious, and troublesome they might be, would have been a very grave humiliation. To hesitate to make a beginning with our own policy of improving the administrative machinery of the Indian Government would have been taken as a sign of nervousness, trepidation and fear; and fear, which is always unworthy in any Government, is, in the Indian Government, not only unworthy, but dangerous. I hope the House concurs with his Majesty's Government.

In answer to a question the other day, I warned one or two of my hon'ble friends that, in resisting the employment of powers to suppress disturbances under the Act of 1818 or by any other lawful weapon we could find, they were promoting the success of that disorder, which would be entirely fatal to all the projects with which they sympathised. The Despatch reached us in due course. It was considered by the Council of India and by His Majesty's Government, and our reply was sent about a fortnight ago. Some one will ask—are you going to lay these despatches on the table to-day? I hope the House will not take it amiss if I say that at this stage—perhaps at all stages—it would be wholly disadvantageous to lay these two despatches on the table. We are in the middle of details and discussion of details to-day, and it would break up the continuity if we had a premature discussion *coram populo*. Every one will understand that discussions of this kind must be very delicate, and it is of the utmost importance that these discussions should be conducted with perfect and entire freedom. But, to use a word that I do not often use, I might adumbrate the proposal.

A "COUNCIL OF NOTABLES."

This is how the case stands. The despatch reached His Majesty's Government, who considered it; and we then set out our views upon the points raised in the despatch. We have left it to the Indian

Government to frame a Resolution, a kind of bill, embodying the submissions or instructions addressed to them by His Majesty's Government. That draft Resolution will in due course be sent here. We shall consider that draft, and then it will be my duty to present proposals to this House if legislation is necessary, as probably will be; and they will then be returned to India to be discussed there by all those concerned. The proposals I would adumbrate are these. We have given approval to the establishment of an Advisory Council of Notables. Those who are acquainted with Indian affairs will recollect that Lord Lytton in 1877 set up a Council of this kind. It was a complete failure.

EARL PERCY:—Was it actually brought into existence?

MR. MORLEY:—I think so, but it never did any good. Lord Curzon had the idea of a Council, but I think the scope was limited to business connected with the Imperial Service Troops. The Council of Notables would have a much wider scope. It would be purely advisory, and would be called together from time to time for the double purpose of eliciting independent opinion and diffusing, what is really the most important thing of all—correct information as to the actions and intentions of the Government. It is remarkable how the Government, on the one hand, knows so little of the mind of the people—and it is just as deplorable on the other hand, that the people know so very little about the mind of the Government. It is a tremendous chasm that we have to bridge; and whether political machinery can ever bridge it, I know not.

LEGISLATIVE CONSTITUTION AND PROCEDURE.

The second proposal is the acceptance of the general principle of a substantial enlargement of the Legislative Council—both the Governor-General's Legislative Council and the Provincial Legislative Councils. Details of this reform have to be further discussed in consultation with the local Governments in India, and an official majority must be maintained. Thirdly, in the discussion of the Budget in the Viceroy's Council, the subjects are to be grouped and explained severally by the members of the Council in charge, and a longer time—this is a thing often demanded—is to be allowed for detailed discussion and general debate.

INDIANS IN THE COUNCIL OF INDIA.

I should like to add one more conclusion that I have not arrived at without deliberation and consideration. The Secretary of State has the privilege of nominating members of the Council of India. I think the time has now come when the Secretary of State may safely, wisely and justly nominate one, or it may be two, Indian members. I will not discuss the question now. I may have to come to Parliament for legislation at a later stage: but I think it right to say that this is my intention. It oppresses me to think how few opportunities, either in India or here, the governing bodies have of hearing the views of the Indian people.

THE TRUE SECRET OF GOVERNMENT.

I think I have defended myself from ignoring the principle that there is a difference between the Western European and the Indian Asiatic. That is a vital difference, and it is infatuation to ignore it. But there is another vital fact—namely, that the Indian Asiatic is a man with very vivid susceptibilities of all kinds, and with great traditions, with long traditions of a civilisation of his own. We are bound to treat him with the same kind of respect and kindness and sympathy that we should expect to be treated with, ourselves. Only the other day I saw by chance a letter from General Gordon to a friend of mine. He wrote: "To govern men, these is but one way, and it is an eternal truth. Get into their skins. Try to realise their feelings. That is true of Government." That is not only a great ethical, but a great political law, and I hope that in all we do, in all this House does, it will not be forgotten.

BRITISH RULE MUST CONTINUE.

It would be folly to pretend to any dogmatic assurance—and I certainly do not—as to the secrets of the future in India. But anybody who takes part in the rule of India, whether as a Minister or as a member of the House of Commons participating in discussion on the affairs of India,—anybody who wants to take a fruitful part in such discussion will, if he does his duty, find himself in the position that British rule will continue, and ought to continue, and must continue. There is, I know, a school—I do not think it has any representative in this House—which says we might wisely walk out of India, and that the Indians would manage their own affairs better than we could manage them for them. I think anyone who pictures to himself the anarchy, the bloody chaos that would follow from any such withdrawal would shrink from any such position. We, at all events—the Ministry and the members of this House—are bound to take a completely different view. I believe that certainly the Government, and certainly this House, in all its parties and groups, are determined that we ought to face, that we do face all these mischiefs, difficulties, and dangers of which I have been speaking with a clear conscience. We know we are not doing it for our own interest, but for the interest of the millions committed to us. We ought to face it with a clear conscience, with sympathy, kindness, firmness, and love of justice, and, whether the weather be fair or foul, in a valiant and hopeful spirit.

SPEECH AT ARBROATH.

[*Mr. Morley, Secretary of State for India, addressed a crowded meeting of his constituents on the 21st October 1907 in the Public Hall, Arbroath, when Provost Alexander presided. Mr. Morley, who on rising met with a most enthusiastic reception, the audience rising and cordially singing "For He's a Jolly Good Fellow," said :—*

MR. PROVOST, LADIES AND GENTLEMEN :—I is an enormous satisfaction to me to find myself once more here, I am afraid the first time since the polling, and since the majority—was it 2,500 ?—(*laughter*)—that splendid majority that these burghs were good enough to give me. I value very much what the Provost has said, when he told you that I have never, though I have had pretty heavy burdens, neglected the local business of Arbroath and the other burghs. (*Cheers.*) The Provost truly said that I hold an important and responsible office under the Crown ; and I hope that fact will be the excuse, if excuse be needed, for my confining myself to-night to a single topic. When I spoke to a friend of mine in London the other day he said, " What are you going to speak about ?" and I told him. He said—and he is a very experienced man—" It is a most uuattractive subject, India." (*Laughter and cheers.*) This is the last place,

Arbroath, and the rest of my constituency, where any apology is needed for speaking about India, because it is you who are responsible for my being Minister for India. If I have been—in many ways I am certain I have been—a deficient Minister, it is your fault. (*Laughter.*) If your 2,500 majority had been 2,500 the other way—a very inconceivable thing I admit—but if it had, I should have been no longer Minister for India. Do you know there is something that strikes the imagination, something that awakens a feeling of the bonds of mankind in the thought that you here and in the other burghs—(shipmen, artificers, craftsmen, and shopkeepers living here)—that you are brought through me, and through your responsibility in electing me, into contact with all these patient millions, hundreds of millions, 300 millions, across the seas. I say that is a fact that strikes the imagination; and therefore it is that I will not make any apology to you to night for talking to you about India, the responsibility for which you are yourselves involved in. Let me say this, not only to you gentlemen here, but to all British constituencies—that it is well you should have patience enough to listen to a speech about India; because it is no secret to anybody who understands these things that, if the Government were to make a certain kind of bad blunder in India,—which I do not expect them to make—there would be short work for a long time to come with many of these schemes, financial schemes, which you have set your heart upon. Do not believe, do not think, if any mishap were to come to pass in India that you can go on with that admirable programme of social reforms, all costing money, in the spirit in which you are now about to pursue it.

HIS CONSISTENCY.

It is not a fantastical or academic theme I present to you; it is a theme in which your own deepest political interests are closely involved. (*Cheers.*) Now, I am not very fond of talking of myself, but there is one single personal word that I would like to say, and this is really the only place—this or one of the other burghs in my constituency—these are the only places in which I should not be ashamed to say that word. But you, after all, are concerned in the consistency of your representative. Now I think a public man who spends much time in vindicating his consistency makes a mistake. I will confess to you in friendly, but strict confidence, that I have winced when I read of lifelong friends of mine saying that I have shelved in certain Indian transactions the principles of a lifetime. One of your countryman said that, like the Python—that fabulous creature who had the largest swallow that any creature ever had—I have swallowed all my principles. I am a little disappointed in some ways. When a man has laboured for more years than I care to count for Liberal principles and for Liberal causes and thinks he may possibly have accumulated a little credit in the bank of public opinion (*cheers*)—and in the opinion of his party and his friends—(*cheers*)—it is a most extraordinary surprise to him to find when he draws a very small cheque upon that capital to find the cheque returned with the uncomfortable and ill-omened words, "No effects." (*Laughter.*) I am not going to argue that I am not going to defend myself. A long time ago a journalistic colleague, who was a little uneasy at some line I took upon this question or that, comforted himself by saying, "Well, well, this (speaking of me) swings on the tide, but the anchor holds." (*Cheers.*) Yes, gentlemen, I am not a Pharisee, but I do believe that my anchor holds. (*Cheers.*)

OUR FIRST DUTY IN INDIA.

Now to India. I observed the other day that a certain Bishop—the Bishop of Lahore—in India said —and his words put in a very convenient form what is in the minds of those who think about Indian questions at all—

> It is my deep conviction that we have reached a point of the utmost gravity and of far reaching effect in our continued relations with this land, and I most heartily wish there were more signs that this fact was clearly recognised by the bulk of Englishmen out here in India, or even by our rulers themselves.

Now you and the democratic constituencies of this kingdom are the rulers of India. You are among them, and it is to you, therefore, that I come to render my account. Just let us see where we are. Let us put this case. When critics assail Indian policy in this question or that, I want to know where we start from? Some of you in Arbroath wrote to me, perhaps a year ago, and called upon me to defend the system of Indian Government and the policy of which I am responsible. I declined, for reasons which I stated at the moment; and I am here to-night to render an account of my stewardship and to answer in anticipation all those difficulties which many people, with whom in many ways I sympathise, feel. Let us see where we start from. Does anybody want me to go to London to-morrow morning, and to send a telegram to Lord Kitchener, who is Commander-in-Chief in India, and tell him that he is to disband the Indian Army, to send home as fast as we can despatch transports, the British contingent of the Army, and bring away the whole of the Civil servants? Suppose it to be true, as some people in Arbroath seemed to have thought—I am not arguing the question—that Great Britain loses more than she gains; supposing it to be true that India would have worked out her own salvation without us; supposing it to be true that the present Government of India has many defects—and I do not know any Government in the world, except the present Cabinet—(*laughter*),—which has not defects —supposing all that to be true, do you want me to send that telegram to Lord Kitchener to-morrow morning to clear out bag and baggage? How should we look in the face of the civilised world if we had turned our back upon our duty and upon our task? How should we bear the savage stings of our own consciences, when, as assuredly we should, we heard through the dark distances the roar and scream of confusion and carnage in India? How should we look in the face of the civilised world, how should we bear the stings of our own consciences? Then people of this way of thinking say "That is not what we meant." What is meant, gentlemen? The outcome, the final outcome, of British rule in India may be a profitable topic for the musings of meditative minds; but we are not here to muse; we have the duty of the day to perform, we have the tasks of to-morrow laid out before us. Now, where do they start from? In the interests of India, to say nothing of our own national honour, in the name of duty and of common sense, our first and commanding task is to keep order and to quell violences among race and creed, and sternly to insist on the impartial application of rules of justice, independent of European or of Indian. We start from that. We have got somehow or other wisely or unwisely, by a right policy or erroneous policy, we have got to maintain order.

Now there are some difficulties in this great task in England, and I am not sure that I will exclude Scotland, but I said England in order to save your feelings. (*Laughter.*) Now, one great difficulty is the difficulty of finding out, of knowing what actually happens. Scare head-lines in the bills of important journals are misleading. I am sure some of you must know the kind of mirror which distorts features, elongates lines, makes round what is lineal, and so forth; and I assure you that a mirror of that kind does not give you a more grotesque reproduction of the human physiognomy than some of these tremendous telegrams give you as to what is happening in India. That is one difficulty, and I could illustrate that if I liked and if you had patience. Another point is that the Press is very often flooded with letters from Indians or *ex*-Indians, letters too often coloured with personal partisanship leaning this way and that. There is a great deal of writing on the Indian Government by men who have acquired the habit while they were in the Government, unluckily retaining the habit after they come home and live, or ought to live, in peace and quietness among their friends here. That is another of our difficulties. But, still, when all these difficulties are measured and taken account of, it is impossible to overrate the courage, the patience and fidelity, with which the present House of Commons has faced a not at all easy moment in Indian Government. You talk of democracy; people say, "Oh! Democracy cannot govern remote dependencies." I do not know; that is a very grave question; but, so far, after one Session of the most Liberal Parliament that has ever sat in Great Britain, this most democratic Parliament so far, at all events, has safely rounded that very difficult angle. (*Cheers.*) It is quite true that in reference to a certain Indian a Conservative member rashly called "Why don't you shoot him?" The whole House, Tories, Radicals, and Labour men, they all revolted against any such doctrine as that; and I augur from the proceedings of the last Session—and next Session may entirely shake me down to the ground, I do not know—but I do augur from the proceedings of the last Session that democracy, in this case at all events, has shown, and I think is going to show, its capacity for facing these enormously difficult and complicated problems. (*Cheers.*)

CANADA AND INDIA.

Now, I sometimes say to friends of mine in the House, and I venture respectfully to say it to you —there is one tremendous fallacy which it is indispensable for you to banish from your minds when you are thinking from the point of view of a British Liberal, to banish from your minds when you think of India. It was said the other day—no, I beg your pardon, it was alleged to have been said—by a British Member of Parliament now travelling in India, and a gentleman I think the more of for having an open mind, willing to hear both sides, anxious to learn before he comes home to teach—he will learn a good deal, and I hope he will communicate the fruits of his teaching to the House of Commons, where I shall be able to examine them. (*Cheers.*) Now I am not at all sure that he said this; but it does not matter, because many other people have said it—That whatever is good in the way of self-government for Canada must be good for India. In my view that is the most concise statement that I can imagine, and the grossest fallacy in all politics. (*Cheers.*) I think it is a most dangerous, I think it is the hollowest and, I am sorry to say, the commonest of all the fallacies in the history of the world in all stages of civilisation. (*Cheers.*) Because a particular policy or principle is true and expedient and vital in certain definite circumstances, therefore it is equally true and vital in a completely different set of circumstances. A very dangerous and gross fallacy. You might just as well say that, because a fur coat in Canada at certain times of the year is a most comfortable garment, therefore a fur coat in the Deccan of India is a sort of handy garment which you might be very happy to wear. (*Laughter.*) You might say, "Oh! but a form of Government is one thing and a coat is another." I only throw it out to you as an example and an illustration. Where the historical traditions, the religious beliefs, the racial conditions are all different—I do not want to be arrogant or insolent—but I say that to transfer by mere logic all the conclusions that you apply to one case to the other is the highest of political folly (*cheers*), and I for one, will never lend myself to that doctrine.

THE ANALOGY OF IRELAND AND INDIA.

You may say, now you are laying down a different law, different rules of policy in India from those which for the best part of your life you laid down for Ireland. Yes, that reproach will have sting in it if you persuade me that Ireland with its history, the history of the Union and so forth, is exactly analogous to the 300 millions of people in India. I am not at all afraid of facing that test. (*Cheers.*) I cannot but remember that in speaking to you I may be speaking to people many thousands of miles away, but all the same I shall speak to you and to them perfectly frankly. (*Cheers.*) I don't myself believe in artful diplomacy; I have no gift for it, to my great misfortune. (*Laughter.*) There are two sets of people you have got to consider. First of all, I hope that the Government of India, so long as I am connected with it and responsible for it to Parliament and to the country, will not be hurried by the anger of the impatient idealist. The impatient idealist—you know him. I know him. (*Hear, hear.*) I like him; I have been one myself. (*Laughter.*) He says, "You admit that so and so is right; why don't you do it—why don't you do it now?" I sympathise with him whether he is an Indian idealist or a British idealist. Ah! gentlemen, how many of the most tragic miscarriages in human history have been due to the impatience of the idealist! (*Loud cheers.*) I should like to ask, to come to detail, the Indian idealist, for example, whether it is a good way of procuring what everybody desires, a reduction of Military expenditure, whether it is a good way of doing that to foment a spirit of strife in India which makes reduction of Military forces difficult, which makes the maintenance of Military force indispensable? It is a good way to help reformers like Lord Minto and myself, to help us to carry through reform, to inflame the minds of those who listen to these teachers, to inflame their minds with the idea that our proposals and projects are shams? I don't think it is. (*Hear, hear.*)

DISORDER AND REPRESSION.

And I will say this, gentlemen. Do not think

there is a single responsible leader of the reform party in India who does not deplore the outbreak of disorder which we have had to do our best to put down, who does not agree that disorder whatever your ultimate policy may be—at any rate, violent disorder must be put down, and that with a firm hand. (*Cheers.*) If India to-morrow became a self-governing Colony—which is the language used by some—disorder would still have to be put down with a firm hand, with an iron hand; and I do not know to whom these gentlemen propose to hand over the charge of governing India. But whoever they might be, depend upon it that the maintenance of order is the foundation of anything like future progress. (*Cheers.*) If any of you hear unfavourable language applied to me as your representative, just remember considerations of that kind. To nobody in this world, by habit, by education, by experience, by views expressed in political affairs for a great many years past, to nobody is repression, exceptional repression, more distasteful. There is the policeman, of course, who, you will all agree, is a form of repression we cannot dispense with; but exceptional repression is no more distasteful to any one than it is to your representative (*Hear, hear, and cheers.*) After all, gentlemen, you would not have me see men try to set the prairie on fire without arresting the hand. You would not blame me when I saw men smoking their pipes—political pipes, or ordinary pipes—smoking pipes near powder magazines, you would not blame me, you would not call me an arch coercionist, if I said, "Away with the men and away with the powder." (*Hear, hear, and cheers.*) We have not allowed ourselves—I speak of the Indian Government—to be hurried into the policy of repression. I say this to what I would call the idealist party, and in spite of nonsense that I read in some quarters that ought to know better, about apathy and supineness. We will not be hurried into repression any more than we will be hurried into the other direction. Then the other party, which finds a very good voice, which is very vocal in this country, say:—"But, oh! we are astonished, and India is astonished, and it is time that India is astonished, and amazed at the licence that you extend to newspapers and to speakers; why don't you stop it?" Orientals, they say, do not understand it. Yes, but just let us look at that. We are not Orientals; that is the root of the matter. We are in India. We English, Scotch and Irish are in India because we are not Orientals; and if I am told that the Oriental view is that they cannot understand that the Press are allowed to write what they like—well, experiments may fail, but, anyhow, that is a Western experiment which we are going to try, not only through this Government, but through other Governments. We are representatives, not of Oriental civilisation, but of Western civilisation, of its methods, its principles, its practices; and I for one will not be hurried into an excessive haste for repression by the argument that Orientals do not understand this toleration.

THE INDIAN GOVERNMENT VIEW.

You will want to know how the situation is viewed at this moment in India itself, by those who are responsible for the Government of India. I think it is best to be quite straightforward, and the view is not a new view at all. The view is that the situation is not at all dangerous, but that it requires serious and urgent attention. (*Cheers.*) That seems to be the verdict, for the moment it is the verdict.

MODERATES AND EXTREMISTS.

Those who are called Extremists are few, but they are active, their field is wide, and their nets are far spread. Anybody who has read history knows that the Extremist beats the Moderate by his fire, his fiery energy, his very narrowness and concentration. So be it; we remember it; and we watch it all, with that lesson of historic experience full in our minds. But still we hold that it would be the height of political folly for us at this moment to refuse to do all we can do to rally the Moderates to the cause of the Government, simply because the policy will not satisfy the Extremists. Let us, if we can, rally the Moderates, and if we are told that the policy will not satisfy the Extremists, so be it; our line will remain the same. This is a great lesson, a great principle, a great maxim. It is the height of folly to refuse to rally Moderates, and what we shall call sensible people, because we will not satisfy Extremists. (*Cheers.*) Now I am detaining you rather unmercifully, but I doubt whether—and do not think I say it because it happens to be my department—of all the questions that are to be discussed now, perhaps for some years to come, any question can be more important than the question of India. There are many aspects of it which it is not possible for me to go into, as, for example, some of its Military aspects; but I certainly doubt whether there is any question more important, more commanding at this moment, and for some time to come, than the one which I am impressing upon you to-night. Is all this what is called unrest in India froth? Is it deep rolling? I urge that if it is froth we shall get the better of it. Is this unrest the result of natural order and wholesome growth in this vast community with its 300 millions of population? Is it natural effervescence, or is it deadly fermentation? Is India with all its heterogeneous populations—is it moved really to new and undreamt of unity? It is the vagueness of the discontent, which is not universal, but of the discontent so far as we can perceive it—it is the vagueness that makes it harder to understand, harder to deal with. Some of them are angry with me. Why? Because I have not been able to give them the moon. (*Laughter.*) I have got no moon, and if I had I would not give them the moon. I would not give anybody the moon because I do not know who lives there. I do not know what kind of conditions prevail. But, seriously, I read pretty carefully—not very pleasing reading—I read much of the Press in which their aspirations are put forth. I think it is my duty to do that.

(*Cheers.*) But I declare to you I cannot find what it is precisely they want us to do which we are not anxious slowly and gradually to make a way for eventually doing. But there must be patience and there must be, whatever else there is, firmness.

A LITERARY DIVERGENCE.

I want, if I may, to make here a little literary divergence. Much of this movement arises from the fact that there is now a considerable, a large, body of educated Indians who have been fed at our instigation, by our means, upon the great teachers and masters of this country—Milton, and Burke, and Macaulay, and John Stuart Mill. I think it is a mistake that we should not feel that these masters should have a great force and influence. They may; but still I am not surprised at all, or you, that these educated Indians who read these great masters and teachers of ours are intoxicated with the ideas of freedom and nationality and self-government which those great writers promulgate. (*Cheers.*) I entirely agree. Who of us can wonder who had the privilege in the days of our youth, at college or at home, of turning over those golden pages and seeing that lustrous firmament dome over our youthful imaginations—who of us can forget, shall I call it the intoxication and rapture, with which we made friends with these truths? (*Cheers.*) Then why should we be surprised that young Indians feel the same movement of mind when they make free use of those great teachers that we put into their hands? (*Cheers.*) I would only say this. I know some of these teachers pretty well. I only say this to my idealist friends, whether Indian or European, that for every passage that they can find in Mill or Burke, or Macaulay, or that splendid man, Bright—(*cheers*)—for every passage they can find in the speeches or writings of these great teachers of wisdom, for every such passage I will find them a dozen passages in which, in the language of Burke, one of those teachers on whom these men rely, gives the warning—"How weary a step do those take who endeavour to make out of a great mass a true political personality!" I believe those are the words of Burke, and they are words that are much to be commended to those zealous men in India—how many a weary step has to be taken before they can form themselves into a mass which has a true political personality! I say all this. It may be wasted, but I do believe anybody who has a chance ought to appeal to the better mind of India, to the better mind of educated India. Time has gone on, experience has widened. I have never lost my invincible faith that there is a better mind in all great communities in the human race—(*cheers*)—and that that better mind, if you can reach it, if statesmen in times to come can reach that better mind and awaken it and evoke it, can induce it to apply itself to practical purposes for the betterment of the conditions of that community, they will indeed have a beneficent fame. There are—nothing strikes me much more than this when I talk of the better mind of India, and there is no use discussing it—there are subtle elements, religious, spiritual, mystical, traditional, historical in what we may call for the moment the Indian mind, which are very hard for the most candid and patient to grasp or to realise the force of; but we have got to try. (*Hear, hear.*) I always remember a little passage in the life of a great Anglo-Indian, Sir Henry Lawrence, a very simple passage, and it is this. "No one ever ate at Sir Henry Lawrence's table without learning to think more kindly of the natives." I wish that at every Anglo-Indian table—I wish I could think that at every Anglo-Indian table to-day nobody has sat down without having learned to think a little more kindly of the natives before leaving it. (*Cheers.*) I will only say one more thing at this point. India is perhaps the one country—bad manners, overbearing manners are very disagreeable in all countries—India is the only country where bad and overbearing manners are a political crime. (*Cheers.*) The Government have been obliged to take measures of repression; they may be obliged to take more. But we have not contented ourselves with measures of repression. I have said, we have never declined to rally the Moderates because the Extremists would not be contented.

THE REFORM SCHEME.

Those of you who have followed Indian matters at all during the last few weeks or months—two or three months—are aware there is a reform scheme, a scheme to bring the Indians closely—giving them a chance, at all events of coming more closely—into contact with the Government of their country. Though the government of India issued certain proposals expressly marked—I should like this to be observed—as provisional and tentative, there was no secret hatching of a new Constitution. Their circular was sent about to obtain an expression of Indian opinion, official and non-official. Plenty of time has been given and is to be given for an examination and discussion of the information. We shall not be called upon to give an official decision until spring next year, and shall not personally be called upon for a decision before the middle of next Session. If you will let me, I will say that we look with satisfaction on the new policy of leaving the Indian protected States and the Indian Princes who rule over them—and they amount to over 60 millions of population outside the area of what is called the British area—to leave these Princes much more to themselves. This is a step we have taken to which I attach the greatest importance. Two Indians have for the first time been appointed to be members of the Council of India sitting at Whitehall. (*Cheers.*) I appointed these two gentlemen, not only to advise the Secretary of State in Council, not only to help to keep him in touch with Indian opinion and Indian interests, but as a marked and conspicuous proof on the highest scale, by placing them on this important advisory and in some respects, ruling body, that we no longer mean to keep Indians at arms' length or shut the door of the Council Chamber of the Paramount Power against them. (*Cheers.*) Let me press this little point upon you.

The root of the unrest, discontent, and sedition, so far as I can make out after constant communication with those who have better chances of knowing the problem at first hand than I could have had—the root of the matter is racial and not political. (*Cheers.*) Now, that being so, it is of a kind that is the very hardest to reach. You can reach political sentiment. Racial dislike, perhaps some would call it in some cases hatred—it is a dislike not of political domination, but of our racial domination; and my object in making that great and conspicuous change in the constitution of the Council of India which advises the Secretary of State for India, my object was to do something—you might say not much—but to do something, and if rightly understood and interpreted to do a great deal, to teach all in India, from the youngest competition—wallah who arrives there that in the eyes of the Government of India the Indian is perfectly worthy—we do not say it is so in words alone, we have now shown it in act—by giving a share in the Council of the Paramount Power.

FAMINE AND PLAGUE.

There is one more difficulty—two difficulties—and I must ask you for a couple of minutes. I only need name them—famine and plague. At this moment, when you have thought and argued on all these political things, the Government of India is a grim business. Now, if there are no rains this month, the spectre of famine seems to be approaching, and nobody can blame us for that. Nobody expects the Viceroy and the Secretary of State to play the part of Elijah on Mount Carmel who prayed for and saw a little cloud like a man's hand until the heavens became black with winds and cloud and there was a great rain. That is beyond the reach of Government. All we can say is that never before was the Government found more ready than it is now to do the very best to face the prospect. Large suspensions of revenue and rent will be granted, allowances will be made to distressed cultivators, and no stone will be left unturned. The plague figures are terrible. At this season plague mortality is generally quiescent; but this year, even if the last three months of it show no rise, the plague mortality will still be the worst that has ever been known, I think, in India's recorded annals. Pestilence during the last nine months has stalked through the land wasting her cities and villages, slaying its millions, uncontrolled and uncontrollable, so far as we can tell, by human forethought or care. When I read some of these figures in the House of Commons, there were considerable loudish cries of "Shame." I felt that these cries came from the natural sympathy, horror, amazement, and commiseration with which we all listen to such ghastly stories. But of course no shame to the Government of India. If you see anything in your newspapers about these plague figures, remember that this is not like an epidemic here. In trying to remedy plague, you have to encounter tremendous habits and prejudices. Suppose you find plague is conveyed (some think it is) by a flea upon a rat, and suppose you are dealing with a population who object to the taking away of life. You see at once the difficulty that has to be encountered. The Government of India have applied themselves with great energy, with fresh activity, and they believe they have got the secret of this fell disaster. They have laid down a large policy of medical, sanitary, and financial aid. (*Cheers.*) I am a tremendous niggard of public money. (*Cheers.*) I watch the expenditure of Indian revenue as the ferocious dragon of the old mythology watched the golden apples. (*Laughter.*) I do not forget that I come from a country which, so far as I have known it, is most generous, if it is also the most prudent. Nevertheless, though I have—both of my own temperament and, I am sure, of the prejudices of my constituents—to be most thrifty, almost parsimonious, upon this matter, the Council of India and myself will, I am sure, not stint or grudge. (*Cheers.*) I can only say, in conclusion, that I think I have said enough to convince you that I am doing what I believe you would desire me to do—approaching, along with admirable colleagues in India and admirable colleagues at home; conducting administration in the spirit which I believe you will approve with impartiality; listening to all I can learn; desirous to support all those who are toiling to do good work in India—(*Cheers*);—and that I shall not, for my part, be deterred from pursuing to the end, as I have persevered in up to this moment, a policy of firmness, of slow reform. We shall not see many fruits of it in our day. Never mind; we shall have made a beginning, and in more than one thing we have made a beginning in firmness, reform, and resolute patience. (*Loud cheers.*)

THE PARTITION OF BENGAL.

On Monday, February 26, 1906, Mr. Herbert Roberts moved the following amendment to the address :—

"But we humbly beg to represent to your Majesty that this House regards with concern the widespread dissatisfaction and unrest in India due to the recent policy of the Government, culminating in the Partition of Bengal, and is of opinion that such modifications should be made in the form of administration in Bengal as will tend to allay the existing discontent; and we further beg to represent to your Majesty that the reasonable demands of the Indian people for a larger share in the administration of their affairs should receive the consideration of the Government."

Mr. Morley made the following speech on the occasion :—

This Parliament presents a considerable number already of new features; and it is a new feature and one, I think, on which we ought to congratulate ourselves, that this afternoon we have had six maiden speeches in succession from gentlemen who have shown themselves possessors of a competent knowledge of Indian subjects, and were eager to express the views which they represented. (*Hear, hear.*) I for one have no quarrel with Mr. Roberts. Though I am not one of those who desire the House of Commons should be always interfering with the complex and difficult affairs of India, yet I think a debate of this kind can do nothing but good. (*Hear, hear.*) Upon the Partition of Bengal I do not propose to detain the House very long. I wish very much for many reasons that Mr. Brodrick was in the House, because he knows better than I can possibly know from the papers what was in the mind of the India Office and what was also in the mind of the Indian Government of that day. So far as my information goes, I cannot assent to the views of those gentlemen who have said that the movement for the Partition of Bengal arose from political motives and from the desire to repress the expression of its political opinion. Whether the original motives may not have taken on some colour of that kind I am not in a position to affirm or deny. But I think Sir H. Cotton almost admitted that there was a case for the re-distribution of the boundaries of the Province of Bengal in the amount of work laid upon the shoulders of the Governor of that province. He quoted in another connection Lord George Hamilton, and I am sure we all extremely regret the absence from our debates of the noble lord. (*Hear, hear.*) Lord George Hamilton had a longer experience at the India Office as Secretary of State than, I think, anybody now living. Lord George in December last said that, so far as he could recollect, with scarcely an exception, he had never come into contact with a Lieutenant-Governor of Bengal who, when pressed, did not at once admit that the work he had to perform was almost an undue strain upon his strength. There was ample evidence that the labours of the Lieutenant-Governors of Bengal were enormous. That is not saying that the specific re-distribution of the administration of Bengal was the wisest that could be devised. Sir H. Cotton, produced his own scheme to-night, and one or two other gentlemen had made suggestions. But this is not the moment for a technical examination of the precise way in which this re-distribution of the administrative areas was carried out. But it was, and remains undoubtedly an administrative operation which went wholly and decisively against the wishes of most of the people concerned. (*Hear, hear.*) It had been said, and unfortunately by an important person in India, that this demonstration of opposition in Bengal was "machine-made opinion," that it was the work of political wire-pullers and political agitators. I have often heard that kind of allegation made before Governments are apt, when an inconvenient storm of public opinion arises, to lay it at the door of political wire-pullers and agitators. (*Hear, hear.*) There are, however, Indian officials of great weight and authority who entirely put aside that insinuation, and who argue that these Calcutta agitators would have had no response from the people they were appealing to if there had not been in the minds of the people a distinct feeling that they were going to suffer a great wrong and inconvenience; and although no doubt the agitators could form and disseminate these views, yet these sentiments and views existed quite independently of any wire-pulling or agitation. That is my own conclusion from reading the papers. But the re-distribution of Bengal is now a settled fact. At this moment there is a great subsidence—it might be only temporary—but there is a subsidence of the feeling against the redistribution; and in face of that it would be very unreasonable to ask the Government to start afresh to re-distribute the areas and incur a new outlay of taxation. (*Hear, hear.*) As Sir Henry Cotton says, India has just had seven years of pomp and pageantry. The time has not yet come to pass any verdict upon the great administration of Lord Curzon. (*Opposition cheers.*) Some find the energy of it feverish; others find it glorious. At some future date the historian of that time will be able to pronounce much more effectively than we can what Lord Curzon's administration has effected and what not. But none of us will deny his fine powers, his great gifts, and his supreme devotion to what he believes to be the public interests. (*Cheers.*) But my own view is that, at the end of his great period, India should now be allowed to take breath. Therefore, we should now move very slowly. I do not think it would be a desirable or even a defensible movement to attempt to reconstruct Bengal or to restore the old distribution of power in that area. Mr. Roberts suggested that there should be an increase in the number of officers on the Executive Council, an increase in the Legislative Council, and that there should be three Natives added to the Council of the

Secretary of State, and that there should be forth-with an advisory board set up in Calcutta.

MR. HERBERT ROBERTS:—No, an advisory board should be set up, not in Calcutta, but in all the districts of India, for purposes of consultation.

MR. MORLEY:—I would point out that these advisory boards would have no responsibility, that all these other changes would need an Act of Parliament, and I doubt whether good results would follow. Whether the partition was a wise thing or not when it was begun, I am bound to say that nothing was ever worse done so far as the disregard which was shown to the feeling and opinion of the people concerned. (*Cheers.*) It is a fundamental principle in any Government in which Englishmen and Scotsmen are concerned that you are bound to consult and take into consideration all the opinions and even the prejudices of those affected. When the scheme was in the first place exhibited to the people of India, it was exhibited bit by bit. The first proposal was, in one direction, to take certain areas; and the second proposal was an extension and alteration of that. The final scheme, in which all these competitive efforts were summed up, was never submitted to the judgment of anybody in Bengal. The result of that was that we saw a storm raised by a plan which was never carried out; and the storm which was so raised raged with just as much violence against the final scheme when it came to be carried out. I think that is a matter which no defender of the late Government will really stand up for. Coming to the last and most important part, in some respects certainly the widest part, of the amendment, I do not think I need say much. I think I gather already that I need not at all assure Hon'ble Gentlemen who represent Indian interests specially, and I need not assure the House, that so long as I have any responsibility for Indian affairs, I shall not be likely to depart from the general principles of Liberalism—Liberalism not in a party sense, but in that sense in which both parties, in my opinion, desire to see India governed. It seems to be sometimes forgotten that India had an ancient civilisation, and that her people are not barbarians. The officials who have had most dealing with them admit, and not only admit but proclaim, that these people have in them admirable material upon which you may by and by—and in this case I do not at all object to the phrase step by step—build up a system under which they shall have a far greater share than they now have in the Government. When this amendment was first put on the paper, it urged that the Government should take the admission of the Natives of India to a greater share in the Government of India into their immediate consideration. The Viceroy has been on his throne, I think, three months, and I have occupied my office a few weeks, with the trivial interlude of a contested election. For me, therefore, to guarantee the immediate taking of this matter into consideration would, I think, hardly be reasonable, and I am glad that the word has disappeared from the amendment. I, for one, shall deprecate in the case of anybody with whom I have any influence, any resort to that rather harsh, rather arrogant, and rather supercilious language towards the people of Bengal which has been used by some from whom I should not have expected it. In the whole field of government there has been enormous activity and energy, no doubt, during the last six or seven years—in education, public works, irrigation, railways, and in regard to the frontier. I am not going into the frontier question now. It was once said that the study of the Apocalypse either found a man mad or made him mad. I sometimes think when I hear endless discussions about the frontier—not by responsible men, but by irresponsible men,—that the North-West Frontier is almost as prejudicial a field of study in creating this state of mind as the Apocalypse has been said to be. My own view can be expressed in a few sentences. Through the zeal of your officers—most honourable for them—for great public works have sometimes gone to excess, so far as I am concerned, there will be no tendency to stay vigorous action on the part of the Government of India in the direction of works which are proved to be, or which there is good reason to expect will be, of a remunerative character. If you want security and strength in India, one of your ways of getting it is to lighten taxation—(*hear, hear*)—and I should look, therefore, in the direction of greater economy in order to lighten taxation. I respond with all the conviction I have in me to the appeal for sympathy. You may call it sentiment if you like, but a man is ill-fitted for the governing of other men if he does not give a large place to the operation of sentiment. (*Cheers.*)

EXCISE ADMINISTRATION.

[*Mr. Morley received at the India Office, in August 1907, a deputation asking for reforms in the Excise Administration of India.*]

Mr. Morley, replying to the deputation, said that he was very much obliged to the deputation for waiting upon him: they were an important body representing a great centre of opinion in this country, and it was not necessary for them to make any apology for coming to see him. The question of local option had been among these mentioned. But they need not have come to persuade him of the virtues of local option. He had always held that doctrine very strongly—as Mr. Lief Jones might remember, he had even sacrificed a Parliamentary seat to the cause—and he held it now. There were a great many English ideas which could not very well or wisely be transported to India, but this was certainly an idea which he hoped would take root there. He confessed he thought it shocking as Mr. Wilson pointed out, that whilst, we were flattering ourselves that we were spreading western civilisation in the East, we were at the same time, by transporting our industrial system to India, and in other ways spreading what was one of the main causes of the ruin of much social happiness. Dr. Mann had said in the course of a very interesting speech, delivered with sincerity and conviction, that they should have another enquiry, and that that was one of the main objects the deputation wish to press upon him. He had urged that they ought to probe the fundamental causes of the growth of this mischievous western practice and habit. But to probe effectively and fundamentally into the growth of a social habit of this kind was not an operation that could be conducted by a mere Government or official enquiry. The roots of social habits were wide and deep. They were obscure, and they were subtle, requiring enormous, prolonged, and penetrating search. If any one asked him to promise an enquiry into the growth of drinking in India, he would say, "Very well it will take ten years to get to the bottom of it." He thought they were applying a wrong scale to the report and proceedings of the Excise Committee. It was not and could not be intended to be anything like an exhaustive or sociological enquiry into the drinking habit. It was an administrative and Government enquiry. Dr. Mann had complained of it as being somewhat meagre in its scope and conclusions, but all or nearly all administrative operations were meagre, if they were measured by abstract standards, or by social and personal enthusiasms. He passed his days in perusing documents that were certainly not succulent or juicy, but they were admirably composed and of great value for the purpose for which they were composed. Mr. Roberts had relieved him, however, from the need of saying more upon that; for he had testified that the recommendations of the Excise Committee were of the utmost value, and even Dr. Mann, who was a little more critical, admitted there was a great deal to be said for them, although they fell short of what he himself would have recommended. The Government of India had adopted and accepted nearly all the recommendations of the Committee—he thought, with one exception—and he was perfectly sure they would see that they were acted upon and carried. He could not, therefore, see that the occasion had yet arisen for a new enquiry and he thought the Government of India would be quite justified in asking him, if he urged them to have another enquiry, to wait and see what came of the present rather copious recommendations of the Excise Committee. Copious those recommendations certainly were, although some might not consider they were exhaustive. He was sorry to disappoint them, but he did not think he could promise them to make a recommendation to the Government of India to make a further enquiry. He would, however, promise to inform the Government of India that he had received with pleasure the deputation, that it represented important opinion and that the objects they had in waiting on him were enforced by statements of fact and reasonable argument. He would take care that they had a report of all that was said, and he was quite certain they would weigh well the effect and force of it. They must not suppose that the Government of India or indeed any other Government was really callous and conscienceless, or had only what was called an official conscience. An official conscience was better than none, and it was the conscience that was proper when dealing with these affairs of State and the government of societies. The official conscience meant—well, he would not detain them by endeavouring to explain what it did mean—(*laughter*). The Government of India had considered, without further enquiry, what were the causes of the undoubted increase in the drinking habits of the people, and they had set forth their views in what struck him as being a thoroughly reasonable manner. They named a large body of conditions—social conditions—which had undoubtedly let to a great consumption of exciting and intoxicating liquor. It was admitted all through that the Government of India was perfectly clear of stain or reproach in having declared its entire sympathy in the decrease of consumption. They threw off, as they were bound to throw off, revenue interests, and they declared in perfectly good language that the most effective method of forwarding the policy of the Government was to make the tax upon liquor as high as it was possible to raise it without stimulating illicit production, to a degree that would increase instead of diminish the total consumption. There was an illustration which was constantly in his mind of Herbert Spencer's, who warned people against the idea that they could make a reform whenever and wherever they liked. He said:—

Take care that you are not producing another evil when you are removing a given mischief. It is as though you have a great plate

of metal with a bulge in it. You come down with a great blow from the hammer of State intervention and the bulge disappears, but it has reappeared at the other end of the plate.

The Government was bound to be careful in what it did. What did they say? They say that the industrial development of India diverted labourers to large towns where they were employed at relatively high wages on exhausting work and where they were at the same time free from the checks afforded by local public opinion in their own villages. This was bound to lead to larger consumption of liquor. When we boasted of the glorious work we did in spreading Western civilisation in India, he never forgot that by spreading our industrial system, with all the mischief that flowed from it among all its many blessings, there was a tremendous counter-balance to those advances in civilisation on which we justly prided ourselves. The Government of India said the same causes produced the same lamentable results in Western countries as they produced there in India. Everybody who had spoken had complained of the Government of India for not adopting the recommendations of the Excise Committee and substituting for the auction system the system of selecting. It was a very difficult question as they all knew by the discussions which had gone on during his lifetime in this island. What was the best system of licensing? Of course, some of them, no doubt, thought the best system would be to have no licences at all. (*Laughter and "hear, hear."*) The Government of India, so far as he understood their views, thought the system recommended and suggested by the Excise Committee would create a vested interest, though it might not do it legally. They knew of that in this country. They knew of Sharp and Wakefield in this country. And they would have Sharp and Wakefield in India if the Government of India were to adopt the Committee's suggestion. Therefore, so far as outside opinion went, he could not but think that the Government of India were on the right track. Be that as it may, it certainly would not be for him to decide it. The Government of India must discuss it with their revenue authorities. Whether they were eventually converted to the view of the Committee or not, or whether they adhered to the auction system would be discovered in due time. He could not himself undertake to exercise any pressure upon them, because the local circumstances were really decisive in these things and made it impossible for any one except those who had been to India to pronounce any definite opinion. That was really all he had got to say. He was always interested in the subject, and he was especially interested in it in reference to India. He would tell the Government of India what had passed that afternoon, and he was sure it would have an effect of making them more zealous in a wise, forward movement for putting down—for it was not a case of permitting temptations in India, but for putting down—the present excess. The people of this island and perhaps of other islands, were not naturally abstainers, but in India they were, and he was sure the Government of India would be as anxious as any of them to prevent the spread of this new and dire additional plague. (*Hear, hear.*)

BRITISH INDIANS IN THE TRANSVAAL.

[The Secretary of State for India received at the India Office, in November 1907, a deputation to introduce to him the two delegates of the British Indian Association of the Transvaal, Mr. M. K. Gandhi and Mr. H. O. Ally, who had gone to England to protest against the Asiatic Law Amendment Ordinance passed by the Transvaal Legislature.]

Mr. Morley, in reply, said he heartily welcomed their presence that day for two reasons. The first was that he always desired to be familiarised with all currents of feeling relating to the great dependency for whose administration he was responsible to Parliament. The second reason was that this was a practical question affecting the good Government of India very closely. The effect upon public opinion in that country of the disabilities imposed upon Indians in South Africa was, and must continue to be, serious. Indians, returning to their native land from South Africa, carried with them the story of the indignities to which they had been subjected, and the result was to stir up strong prejudices. People in India would ask whether it was not want of will, rather than want of power, which led the British Government to stay its hand when it should be raised in the defence of those principles to which his friend, Lord Stanley of Alderley had referred. For his part he thought great praise was due to Mr. Chamberlain for his enunciation of those principles in 1901 and for the great force and emphasis with which he pressed upon the attention of the Colonial Governments concerned the injustice and harshness of their policy towards British Indians. It was a great irony that one of the first matters in relation to imperial interests brought to the notice of the new Government had been the fact, from which they could not get away, that a bar sinister was placed in some British Colonies upon many millions of the King's subjects. (*Cheers.*) Responsible administrators seldom cared to be reminded of great governing principles, but he was glad Lord Stanley had placed the question on that high plane. The views Lord Stanley expressed in this respect might be held by some to be old fashioned, but he for one shared them entirely. Unfortunately, they had not a white sheet of paper whereon to write. Facts must be faced, and in the circumstances all they could do was to keep their principles in mind and to go as near as they possibly could to their practical application, having regard to all the circumstances. What, then, was the position of the India Office in this matter? It had been recognised by Sir Lepel Griffin that the Minister primarily concerned was not himself, but Lord Elgin. He had been asked by Sir M. Bhownaggree to use his influence with Lord Elgin in favour of appointing a Royal Commission. A serious difficulty in the way of this proposal was that in May next, as the Government hoped, the Transvaal would enter upon the possession of responsible Government. It would surely be an odd preliminary to this grant to create a Commision of enquiry whose recommendations might come into direct conflict with the views of the people on whom the right of self-government was being conferred. It had been said that such a Commission would "solve the question." After prolonged experience of public life he doubted whether he could recall the name of any Commission which had solved any question; and in the circumstances the one proposed would certainly not be favourably situated for arriving at a satisfactory conclusion. It would quite probably mean a collision with the newly-organised Government at the very outset of its career. The plain fact was that we could not dictate to the self-governing Colonies. We could plead, we could argue, we could press for the application of our pinciples. Whether at the Colonial Conference next year, or by the despatches under Lord Elgin's signature, the Government could, and, no doubt, would bring the wider Imperial aspects of this question to the notice of the Colonial authorities, and would use all reasonable arguments. He would remind them that Viceroy after Viceroy had done their best in this matter. Lord Lansdowne's views, as expressed at Sheffield just after the outbreak of the war, had been quoted that day, and reference had been made to the despatches of Lord Elgin when he was in India. As for Lord Curzon, he had carried on a tremendous battle for our Indian fellow-subjects. Proceeding to quote from the seventh Budget speech of the ex-Viceroy as to the demands ineffectively pressed upon representatives of the Natal Government who went out to India with a view to obtaining further supplies of indentured labour, Mr. Morley said that the quotation showed that Natal had refused the conditions laid down by Lord Curzon, and it remained to be seen whether the Transvaal would be more amenable to the requests of Lord Elgin. He was glad to understand that the feeling of many of the white colonists was not unfavourable to the Indians. It was not, after all, very unnatural of the small white shopkeeper to exert whatever influence he might possess with the governing classes in the country to keep out very formidable competitors. He could even understand Indians already in the country desiring to keep out immigrants from their native land who might enter into competition with them. But what he could not understand was mere prejudice and insistence on a principle of racial inferiority, seeing that there were many Indians in the Transvaal pursuing professional or mercantile callings who were greatly superior in many of the elements which made up a civilised being to some of those who were readily admitted into the country. (*Cheers.*) The notion that Indians already there should be subjected to any new disabilities and to new elements of humiliation was one which, he confessed, stirred his feelings deeply, as Lord Lansdowne's were stirred by the treatment of

Indians under the Boer regime. (*Cheers.*) It was a factor in the case not to be overlooked, however, that in some instances we could more effectively demonstrate with foreign powers (as we remonstrated with the Boer Republic) than with our own people in the colonies. (*Shame.*) However, that was a wide field into which he had been tempted by the remarks of Lord Stanley, and all he had now to do was to give them assurances of his sympathetic help. Whatever could be done when the time came in the way of energetic protest against the continuance of any unnecessary disability would be done by the India Office. They might be quite sure he would not be at all slack in backing up the Colonial Office, or possibly in going a little in front. (*Cheers.*)

THE NEED FOR REFORM.

[*On the* 31*st January* 1908, *Dr. Rutherford rose to move as an amendment to the Address, at the end to add:—" But humbly submits that the present condition of affairs in India demands the immediate and serious attention of His Majesty's Government; that the present proposals of the Government of India are inadequate to allay the existing and growing discontent; and that comprehensive measures of reform are imperatively necessary in the direction of giving the people of India control over their own affairs." Mr. Morley said :—*]

I think the House will allow me to preface the few remarks I have to make by informing the House of the decision arrived at by Transvaal Government in respect to the question of Asiatics.

BRITISH INDIANS IN THE TRANSVAAL.

Everybody in the House is aware of the enormous and even passionate interest which has been taken in this subject, especially in India and for very good reasons. Without further preface, let me say this is the statement received by Lord Elgin from the Government of the Transvaal last night :—

Gandhi and other leaders of the Indian and Chinese communities have offered voluntary registration in a body within three months, provided signatures only are taken of educated, propertied, or well-known Asiatics, and finger-prints of the others, and that no question against which Asiatics have religious objections be pressed. The Transvaal Government have accepted this offer, and undertaken, pending registration,

not to enforce the penalties under the Act against all those who register. The sentences of all Asiatics in prison will be remitted to-morrow.

Lord Selborne adds: "This course was agreed to by both political parties." I am sure that in every quarter of the House that will be very welcome news. (*Cheers.*) I do not like to let the matter drop without saying a word—I am sure Lord Elgin would like me to say it—in recognition of the good spirit which the Transvaal Government has shown from the beginning in this very troublesome and difficult episode, and the good end which they have accelerated.

INDIA AND PARLIAMENT.

In reference to the amendment now before the House, I have listened to the debate with very keen, lively, and close interest. I am not one of those who have ever complained of these grave topics being raised whenever opportunity offered in this House. On the whole, looking back over my Parliamentary lifetime, which is now pretty long, I think there has been far too little Indian discussion. (*Cheers.*) Before I came there were powerful minds like Mr. Fawcett and Mr. Bradlaugh and others who did raise Indian questions in a very serious and practical way, though I do not at all commit myself to the various points of view that were then adopted. I am not going to ask members to vote for the Government on that ground. But I do submit that His Majesty's present Government in the Indian department has the confidence both of this House and of the country. (*Cheers.*) I think we have. A very important suggestion was made by Mr. Hart-Davies that a Parliamentary Committee should sit—I persume a joint committee of the two Houses—and my hon'ble friend who spoke last (Mr. Herbert Roberts) said that the fact of the existence of that committee would bring Parliament into closer contact with the mind of India. Well, ever since I have been at the India Office, I have rather inclined in the direction of one of the old Parliamentary Committees, but I will not argue the question now. I can only assure my hon'ble friends that the question has been considered by me, and I see what its advantages might be, but I also perceive very serious disadvantages that there might also be. In these old days they were able to command the services of those Indian Committees, of members of this House and members of another place who had had good experience of administration of one sort and another, and I am doubtful, considering the pre-occupations of public men, whether we should now be able to call a large body of experienced administrators to sit on one of those Committees. And then I would point out another disadvantage. You would have to call away from the performance of their duties in India a great body of men whose duties ought to occupy, and I believe do occupy, all their minds and all their time. But it is an idea, and I do not entirely banish it from my own mind. (*Hear, hear.*)

DEMOCRACY AND THE SETTLED FACT.

Two very interesting speeches—very significant speeches—have been made this afternoon. One was made by my hon'ble friend the mover, and the other was made by the hon'ble member for East Leeds (Mr. O'Grady.) These two speeches, in my respectful judgment, raise a very important issue. I will explain my meaning. Mr. O'Grady has said that democracy was entirely opposed to, and would resist, the doctrine of the settled fact. He says democracy will have nothing to do with settled facts, though he did not quite put it as broadly as that. Now, if that be so, I am very sorry for democracy. (*Laughter.*) I do not agree with my hon'ble friend. I think democracy will be just as reasonable as any other sensible form of government, and I do not believe democracy will for a moment think that you are to rip up a settlement of an administrative or constitutional question because it jars with some abstract *a priori* idea. I for one certainly say that I would not remain at the India Office, or any other great and responsible departmental office, on condition that I made short work of settled facts, and brought in my catalogue of first principles, and arranged the duties of government on those principles. No; nothing would induce me to do it; I would cut off my right hand rather than I would go into any administrative office on any such principles. (*Cheers.*)

"IMPATIENT IDEALISTS."

Then there is my hon'ble friend the member for Brentford. Dr. Rutherford has quarrelled with an expression of mine used in a speech in the country—at Arbroath—about the impatient idealist, and he reproved me for saying that some of the worst tragedies of history had been wrought by the impatient idealists. He was kind enough to say that it was I, among other people, who had made him an idealist, and therefore I ought not to be ashamed of my spiritual and intellectual progeny. (*Laughter.*) I certainly have no right whatever to say that I am ashamed of my hon'ble friend, who made a speech full of interesting views, full of visions of a possible future, and I do not quarrel with him for making that speech. I thought it very interesting, and I believe—I will make him a present of this—that those views are not at all without support among the people of this country. My hon'ble friend said that he was for an Imperial Duma. The hon'ble gentleman has had the advantage of a visit to India, which I have never had. I think he was there for six whole weeks. (*Laughter.*) His Imperial Duma was to be elected, as I understood, by universal suffrage.

DR. RUTHERFORD :—No, not universal suffrage. I said educational suffrage, and also pecuniary suffrage—taxpayers and ratepayers.

MR. MORLEY :—In the same speech the hon'ble gentleman made a grave charge against our system of education in India—that we had not educated them at all; therefore, he excludes at once an enormous part of the population. The Imperial Duma, as I understood from him, was to be subject to the veto of the Viceroy. We are to send out from Great Britain, once in five years, a Viceroy who is to be confronted by an Imperial Duma, just as the Tsar is confronted by the Duma in Russia. Well, that is not my idea of a democracy. Dr. Rutherford has told the House that he visited the State of Baroda, and thought it well governed. Well, there is no Duma there. I will speak quite frankly my own opinion.

"IF I HAD TO FRAME A NEW SYSTEM—"

If I had to frame a new system of Government for India, I declare I would twenty times rather multiply the Baroda system of Government rather than have an Imperial Duma and Universal Suffrage. The speech of my hon'ble friend, with whom I am sorry to find myself, I will not say in collison, but at difference, illustrates what is to my mind one of the grossest of all the fallacies in practical politics—namely that you can cut out, frame, and shape a system of Government for communities with absolutely different sets of social, religious, and economic conditions—that you can cut them all out by a sort of standardised pattern and say what is good for us here, the point of view, the line of argument, the method of solution—that all these things are to be applied right off to a community like India. I must tell him that I think that is a most fatal and mischievous fallacy, and I am bound, after what I have said, to say that I do not think that it is at all involved in Liberalism. Hon'ble members opposite will forgive me if I address a domestic word or two. (*Opposition laughter.*) I have had the good fortune and honour and privilege to have known some of the great Liberals of my time, and there was not one of those great men, Mazzini, Gambetta, Bright, Mr. Gladstone, anybody you like, who would have accepted for a single moment the doctrine on which he really bases his visionary proposition for a Duma. Is there any rational man who says, that if you can lay down political principles and maxims of Government that apply equally to Scotland or to England, or to Ireland, or to France or to Spain, therefore they must be true for the Punjab and the United Provinces?

DR. RUTHERFORD:—I quoted Mr. Bright as making the very proposal I have made, with the exception of the Duma—namely, provincial Parliaments.

MR. MORLEY:—I am afraid I must traverse my hon'ble friend's description of Mr. Bright's view, with which, I think, I am pretty well acquainted.

MR. BRIGHT ON THE RIGHT TRACK.

Mr. Bright was I believe, on the right track at the time in 1858 when the Government of India was transferred to the Crown; but I do not think he was a man very much for Imperial Dumas. (*Laughter.*) He was not in favour of Universal Suffrage—he was rather old-fashioned—(*laughter*)—but Mr. Bright's proposal was perfectly different from that of my hon'ble friend. Sir Henry Maine and others who had been concerned with Indian affairs came to the conclusion that Mr. Bright's idea was right—that to put one man, a Viceroy, assisted as he might be with an effective Executive Council, in charge of such an area as

India and its 300 millions of population, with all its different races, creeds, modes of thought was to put on one man's shoulder a load which no man, of whatever powers, however gigantic they might be, could be expected effectively to deal with. (*Hear, hear.*) My hon'ble friend and others who sometimes favour me with criticisms in the same sense seem to suggest that I am a false brother, that I do not know what Liberalism is. I think I do, and I will even say that I do not think I have anything to learn of the principles or maxims, aye, or of the practice of Liberal doctrines even from my hon'ble friend. (*Opposition laughter and cheers.*) You have got to look at the whole mass of the great difficulties and perplexing problems connected with India from a common-sense plane, and it is not common sense, if I may so without discourtesy, to talk of Imperial Dumas.

AN "ENORMOUS IMPROVEMENT," IN THE POSITION.

I have not had a word of thanks from anybody, in the midst of the present shower of reproach, for what I regard, in all its direct and indirect results and bearings, as one of the most important moves that has been made in connection with the relations between Great Britain and India for a long time—namely, the admission of two Indian gentlemen to the Council of the Secretary of State. (*Hear, hear.*) My hon'ble friend, Mr. Smeaton, wants me to appoint an Indian gentleman to the Viceroy's Executive Council. Well, that is a different thing; but I am perfectly sure that, if an occasion offers, neither Lord Minto nor I would fall short of some such application of democratic principles. The Viceroy I have found as eager for reform and improvement, as acute in reading the situation which has been described so eloquently by some of my hon'ble friends to night, as any of us. (*Hear, hear.*) In itself it is something that we have a Viceroy and a Secretary of State thoroughly alive to the great change in temperature and atmosphere that has been going on in India for the last five or six years, and I do not think we ought to be too impatiently judged. We came in at a rather perturbed time; we did not come into perfectly smooth waters. It is notorious that we came into enormous difficulties which we had not treated. How they were created is a long story which has nothing whatever to do with the present discussion. But what I submit with the utmost confidence is that the situation to-day is an enormous and extraordinary improvement on the situation which we found when we came into office two years ago. (*Hear, hear.*) There have been heavy and black clouds over the Indian horizon during those two years. By our policy those clouds have been gradually dispersed. I am not so unwise as to say that the clouds will never come back again. Nobody who has ever thought at close quarters of the relations between India and this country would ever say that we will never have a great bank of clouds again. It cannot be otherwise; but what has been done by us has been justified, in my opinion, by the event.

THE DEPORTATIONS.

Some fault was found, and I do not in the least wonder at it, with the deportation of two Indian gentlemen. I do not quarrel with the man who finds fault with that proceeding. To take anybody, and deport him without bringing any charge against him and with no intention of bringing him to trial, is a thing which, I think, the House is perfectly justified in calling me to account for. I have done my best to account for it, and to-day any one who knows the Punjab would agree that, whatever may happen at some remote period, its state is exceedingly quiet and satisfactory. I am not going to repeat my justification of that very strong measure of deportation, but I should like to read to the House the words of the Viceroy in the Legislative Council about those circumstances. He said addressing Lord Kitchener:—

> I hope that your Excellency will, on my behalf as Viceroy and as representing the King, convey to His Majesty's Indian troops my thanks for the contempt with which they have received the disgraceful overtures which I know have been made to them. The seeds of sedition have been unscrupulously scattered throughout India, even amongst the hills of the frontier tribes. We are grateful that they have fallen on much barren ground, but we can no longer allow their dissemination.

Will anybody say that, in view of the possible danger pointed to in that language of the Viceroy two or three months ago, we did wrong in using the Regulation which applied to the case? No one can say what mischief might have followed if we had taken any other course than that which we took. (*Hear, hear.*)

THE SIMLA "REFORMS."

Now as to the reforms that are mentioned in my

Hon'ble friend Dr. Rutherford's amendment. It is rather an extraordinary amendment. It submits that "the present condition of affairs in India demands the immediate and serious attention of His Majesty's Government." I can cordially vote for that —(*laughter*)—only remarking that the Hon'ble Member must think the Secretary of State, and the Viceroy, and other persons immediately concerned in the Government of India very curious persons if he supposes that the state of affairs in India does not always "demand their immediate and very serious attention." (*Hear, hear.*) Then the amendment says, "the present proposals of the Government of India are inadequate to allay the existing and growing discontent." I hope it is not presumptuous to say so, but I should have expected a definition from my hon'ble friend of what he thinks these proposals are. I should like to set him a little examination paper. I have studied them a great deal, but would rather not be examined for chapter and verse; but after his travels of six weeks he knows all about them and the state of affairs for which they are the inadequate remedy. I do not want to hold him up as a formidable example; but in his speech to-day he went over—and it does credit to his industry—every single one of the most burning and controversial question of the whole system of Indian government and seemed to say, "I will declare how far this is wrong and what ought to be done with so and so." I think I have got from him 20 *ipse dixits* on all these topics on which we at the India Office are tearing ourselves to pieces. I can assure the hon'ble gentleman that in dealing with India you will fare very ill if you do not listen to the experts. (*Hear, hear.*) When it is said, as I often hear it said, that I, for example, am falling into the hands of our officials, it should be remembered that those gentlemen who go to India get into the hands of other people.

DR. RUTHERFORD:—I was in the hands of both officials and Indians.

MR. MORLEY :—Then the Hon'ble Member came out of the hands of both of them still with something to learn. (*Laughter and cheers.*) I wonder whether, when this House is asked to condemn the present "proposals of the Government of India as being inadequate to allay the existing and growing discontent," it is realised exactly how the case stands. I will repeat what I said in the debate on the Indian Budget as to how the case stands. The Government of India sent over to the India Office their proposals—their various schemes for Advisory Councils and so forth. We at the India Office subjected them to a careful scrutiny and laborious examination. As a result of this careful scrutiny and examination they were sent back to the Government of India with the request that they should submit them to discussion in various quarters. The instruction to the Government of India was that by end of March the India Office was to hear what the general view was at which the Government of India had themselves arrived upon all those plans, complexities and important variations. We wanted to know what they would tell us. When the scheme is again sent home, it will be for us at the India Office to consider how far the report so arrived at, how far these proposals so ripened by Indian opinion, carry out the policy which His Majesty's Government have in view. Surely that is a reasonable and simple way of proceeding. When you have to deal with complex communities of varied races and all the other peculiarities of India, you have to think out how your proposals will work. Democracies do not always think how things will work.

EXECUTIVE AND JUDICIAL FUNCTIONS.

My hon'ble friend, Sir Henry Cotton, made a speech which interested me by its moderation and reasonableness. He made a number of remarks in perfect good faith about officials which I receive in a chastened spirit, for he has been for a very long time a very distinguished official himself. (*Opposition laughter.*) Therefore he knows all about it. (*More laughter.*) He went on to talk of the great problem of the separation of the executive and judicial functions, which is one of the vital problems of India. I can only assure my hon'ble friend that that is engaging our attention both in India and here. It may fall to my lot at some future time to speak of it. Another of the subjects to which the hon'ble member referred and to which the attention of the Indian Government has been specifically directed, has regard to the mitigation of flogging, the restriction of civil flogging, and the limitation of military flogging to specific cases.

"MY HEART IS WITH THE PEOPLE OF INDIA."

My hon'ble friend appealed at the end of his speech to me, saying that all will be well in India if the the Secretary of State make a statement which will show the Indian people that, in his relations with them, his hopes for them, and his efforts for them, he is moved by a kindly, smypathetic, and friendly feeling, showing them that his heart is with them. All I have got to say is that I have never shown myself anything else. (*Hear, hear.*) My heart is with them. What is bureaucracy to me ? To me it is a great machine in India, rather a splendid machine, for performing the most difficult task that ever was committed to the charge of any nation. (*Cheers.*) But show me where it fails—that it is perfect in every respect no sensible man, would contend for a moment—but show me at any point, let any of my hon'ble friends show me from day to day as this session passes, where this bureaucracy as they call it, has been at fault. Do they suppose it possible that I will not show my recognition of that fault and do all that I can to remedy it ? Although the Government of India is very complicated and intricate, they cannot suppose that I shall fail for one moment in doing all in my power to demonstrate to those who live in India that I am moved by a kindly' a sympathetic and a friendly spirit. (*Cheers.*)

THE CONDITION OF INDIA.

[The following speech was delivered in the House of Lords on 30th June 1918 in reply to Lord Curzon's speech, calling attention to the state of India. Viscount Morley of Blackburn, who was cheered on rising, said:—]

My Lords,—I feel that the noble Lord has in many parts of his speech said nothing from which I could in the slightest degree differ. The active and prominent part which he took in the administration of India for six or seven years gives him a title to speak on India which, if it were not for my office, I do not possess. But I do not see why the noble Lord should have wound up with an appeal to me as Secretary of State to be quite sure to resist sedition and to preserve order. Any one who is familiar with the history of Indian administration in the 2½ years during which I have been responsible for it, will do me the justice to say that I have never allowed anything, either popularity in the House of Commons or popularity among my own friends outside the House of Commons, to turn me for one moment by a hair's breath from any action or policy that I thought was required. (*Cheers.*) The noble Lord has said that the introduction of this motion has my entire concurrence. This is quite true, but at the same time I am seriously disappointed at the tone adopted by the noble Lord on one or two points. I will only say now that I think the noble Lord has not been quite careful to remember that we who are here to-night are not the only participants in the debate. There are keen and vigilant listeners in many quarters. There are of course the officers of His Majesty's Government in Simla, there are the political parties in India, those who are called the Moderates and the Extremists and the European community in India. They are all listeners. There are also persons who listen in the fastnesses of Kabul, and every word spoken to-night by the noble Lord will find its way in a few days to Kabul. I think the noble Lord has forgotten those things—I think he has forgotten that we are a responsible Government, and that we have to consider whether the language used or the measures adopted by us tend to play into the hands of those opponents of all possible or serious reform who are looking on our Government with a sinister gleam in their eyes and infatuated dreams in their hearts. The language used by the noble Lord will be thought by such men to be helpful to them against their moderate rivals.

IMPORTANCE OF INDIAN QUESTIONS.

I agree with the noble Lord that this is one of the foremost questions that can engage the attention of the British Parliament. In my view, after considerable experience of responsibility, the question of India stands in the very front rank; along with two or three other questions, such as national defence, the relations with the Colonies, and financial matters.

You can name no front-rank question with which India is not on a perfect level in its claim to vigilant and serious attention. I know your Lordships entirely agree with that. I do not go as far as the noble Lord who once said that he 'was more proud, or as proud, of being a citizen of the country which had had done the greatest thing ever done—that is, had established English rule in India—as he was of being a citizen of the country that defeated the Spanish Armada and produced Hampden and Pitt. I cannot read history in that light. What does it mean? This is not an entirely idle or theoretical digression. It means that it was no grand thing to have beaten back the dark and bigoted power of Spain in the 16th century from our shores and in the 17th century to have founded institutions and laid down principles which are not only the glory of our own country, but which have been made the model and example for the whole civilised world; and, thirdly, to have established the supremacy of England, as Pitt did, over France, in North America, with all the tremendous issues involved in that transaction. While I have every desire to think well of heroic shades, I think it indicates defects in the noble Lord's point of view when he places those achievements on a level with the achievements, grand as they were, of Clive and Warren Hastings and Lord Wellesley. That shows the noble Lord to what a degree the sense of duty in this country has kept alive these great traditions and achievements. When the noble Lord began by saying that

India ought to be outside all party considerations, I began to be suspicious, because I have always observed in my political experience that when gentlemen disclaim the possibility of a party attitude, they very soon find themselves in a severely party attitude. *(Cheers.)* I am bound to say that I see no difference whatever in the tone and spirit and method and tactics of the noble Lord on this most grave subject from the spirit and method of any ordinary party debate. *("Hear hear," and Opposition dissent.)*

LORD CURZON OF KEDLESTON:—I am in the recollection of the House. I made no sort of party or debating attack on the noble Viscount at any point. I rendered him the most cordial and sincere recognition of his services as Secretary of State and his attitude on all Indian questions. I promised, as far as my support is worth anything, my most sympathetic consideration. Really, to hear that my speech was animated by a party attitude is just as great a travesty of my position as is the account of my views of the Armada and the Government of India which the noble Viscount has given. *(Cheers.)*

VISCOUNT MORLEY:—Well, the House must, of course, judge what is and what is not party criticism; and, after all, I am not at all surprised, because the greatest party struggles in all our history have taken place on Indian subjects within comparatively recent date. Now, my Lords, the noble Lord, in talking of the sources of mischief to which Indian peace is exposed and the sources of annoyance and trouble to which Indian officers are exposed, mentioned questions in the House of Commons, and he made the very remarkable statement that such questions were fatal or deleterious. Nobody now living has more reason than myself to dislike the questioning which has gone on for the last two-and-a-half years, but it has not had the slightest significance or importance. It has taken up a certain amount of my time, and of the time of some of my officers, but not a very great amount; but does anybody suppose that democracy is going to be without its simpletons? (*Laughter*) Perhaps not even an aristocracy is without its simpletons. (*Renewed laughter.*) When the noble Lord lays down the tremendous proposition that the Parliamentary system is incompatible with the maintenance of our power in India,

LORD CURZON OF KEDLESTON:—I am very sorry to interrupt, but I did not lay down anything so absurd as that. So far from deprecating questions, the noble Lord will remember that I used to revel in them in the House of Commons. All I did say was that the duty of answering them often imposed a heavy and unreasonable burden on the District Officers in India.

VISCOUNT MORLEY:—The noble Lord used some expression about the Parliamentary system which implied that it was incompatible with the maintenance of order in India. I am glad I was mistaken. However, I was going to ask him, and I do ask him, if he dislikes Parliamentary action, whether in another place or in this House, what are you going to do with your Parliamentary system? It is all very well for the noble Lord sitting there, now free from all responsibility; but, if he was sitting on this side of the House, he would feel that he had to carry on with a Parliamentary system in one way or another. I rather think he indulged in cheap and unworthy irony as to the literary sources of these questioners, and some of their friends in England—Mill and Burke, and some contemporary writers. What are you going to do? Are you going to prevent them reading Mill and even contemporary writers? The noble Lord does not seem to see that we are face to face with an immensely difficult problem, and that the conditions are fixed on us. I agree that Macaulay and those other great men who made education in India what it is are responsible for a great deal of what has happened since. What the noble Lord's achievements were in the field of education, I cannot accurately criticise; but I feel this assuredly, that any Government or Viceroy who takes in hand at the roots the present condition of unrest, will devote all the powers of his mind to the revision of the education system.

THE PARTITION OF BENGAL.

The noble Lord spoke of the Partition of Bengal. Now, I have never for my own part indulged in any of the accusations of which he has complained, and the refutation of which appears to have been his main object in bringing forward this not very fruitful discussion. The Partition of Bengal was a proceeding, I thought, mistaken in its methods, but no language has ever fallen from my lips that has in any way shaken the conclusion that the Partition of Bengal was a settled fact, so far as I am concerned. (*Opposition cheers.*) I will say without any danger of being misunderstood that, when I consider all the circumstances under which the Partition was made—it was a matter of adjusting boundaries and operations of that kind—I could never see why it should have been regarded as so sacrosanct. It may be it is so, and for me it is so because it has become a test, and by that test I am willing to abide so far as I am concerned. But the noble Lord rather surprised me and Lord Ampthill when he said that he returned to India from his stay in England in 1904-5 and accepted without question what he found. I have been informed, and I believe rightly, that, while Lord Ampthill and Sir A. Fraser, the Lieutenant-Governor of Bengal, were hammering out the final scheme of readjustment of boundaries at every stage, the noble Lord had communications made to him on every single particular from time to time. (Viscount Curzon dissented.) I must leave the noble Lord and the noble Lord behind him to settle that between them, and I hope that they will be able to do so. Now, as to Sir Bampfylde Fuller, the acceptance of whose resignation by the Government with regard to the Partition of Bengal, the noble Lord has so severely criticised—I have the pleasure of knowing Sir Bampfylde Fuller; I have had more than one conversation with him, and have a great opinion of his gifts; but I am bound to say that I read with surprise a letter published by him the other day in the *Times* newspaper headed "J' accuse" and attacking Lord Minto and, in a lesser degree, and with a good deal of innuendo, myself. Now, Sir Bampfylde Fuller is a clever and distinguished man who has held high office in Indian Government. What does he do? He takes this moment of all others, when there is a Viceroy at Simla manfully struggling with enormous difficulties which nobody is better able to measure than the noble Lord opposite, to pour into the columns of the English Press what I cannot but call a vitriolic attack on that office. The noble Lord may defend him as he likes. I rather wonder that he should. He says we were wrong in accepting his resignation. Were we wrong? Is it really to be submitted to this House that, whenever a Lieutenant-Governor or anybody else cannot have his own way, he is to threaten the Viceroy with resignation. I do not think that there has ever been a man who has occupied the position of Viceroy who would more stubbornly resist any such action than the noble Lord himself. If I had been in the position of a Lieutenant-Governor, I would never have sent in my resignation to him, because I am perfectly certain it would have been immediately accepted. (*Laughter.*) I can only say for my part, that so long as I am concerned with the Indian Government, if anybody tenders his resignation because he cannot have his own way against the deliberately formed views of his superior authorities, that resignation will be promptly and peremptorily accepted. (*Hear, hear.*) The noble Lord says that disastrous effects followed the acceptance of Sir Bampfylde Fuller's resignation. That is entirely opposed to the facts. I do not think I can publicly name my authority; but, if I tell the noble Lord privately, he will agree that better authority there could not be. This is what I understand to have been the result on the spot of the acceptance of the resignation :—

There was great jubilation in certain journalistic quarters in Calcutta, but no increased violence followed. As to insolence to Europeans, it almost entirely ceased, and when Sir A. Fraser, his successor, went to Dacca some three months later, nothing of the kind took place. Nor has anything been heard of any recrudescence.

It is not, perhaps, particularly wise in me to say that, because I shall be told by-and-by that my words are an inducement to violence. It is quite untrue to say that the resignation caused any violence. The measure was an act of most salutary discipline, and in similar circumstances, I should take the same course.

FRONTIER POLICY.

Now about the frontier policy. We have had two large or considerable frontier enterprises. Both have been conducted with extraordinary military skill and efficiency—(*cheers*),—and have been entirely successful. We have not had what the Government of Lord Elgin had some years ago—we have had no conflagration along that dangerous frontier, because we adhered closely to the policy first laid down by Lord George Hamilton that we would not annex or occupy any portion of tribal territory. That, really, was the secret of the success of both those great expeditions. No policy could have been more loyally and faithfully followed by the Generals in command, and by those who directed those Generals, than was our policy in this case. While I remember what has been said about military autocracy, I am bound to say that there was in this case nothing of that kind. Lord Salibury once said one must beware of soldiers, for they would advise you to make a campaign in the moon lest we should be overrun from the planet Mars. (*Laughter.*) For my part, I shall have no difficulty from anything of that kind. I must really ask your Lordships to pardon me if I do not follow the noble Lord closely, or, indeed, at all, through the Afghan portion of his speech. I wish he could have felt it consistent with his duty to leave the Afghan field as much as possible. There will be plenty of time by and by to look around. Let us wait. The noble Lord talked of our reception of the Amir in India last year. He implied that we ought to have taken advantage of that visit to strengthen our position with that ruler and to make him feel that we had conferred various favours on him —subsidies and the rest, enumerated by the noble Lord—and that these imposed upon him a corresponding duty. We did not say a word to the Amir during his very joyful visit to India about reciprocal duties to us or any other duties; and when the Amir went back from India he went without a single element of friction in his mind, and the good effects of our policy of leaving this powerful man to his own course was shown by what happened on the frontier. It is quite true that Afghans did engage in those expeditions, especially in the Mohmand expeditions; but when things became dangerous, the Amir, to the best of our knowledge and belief, from his correspondence with the Viceroy and in other ways, did his very best, especially in the later stage of the Mohamand expedition, to act in that spirit of friendship which we thought, and rightly thought, to cement during his stay in India. (*Cheers.*)

THE ANGLO—RUSSIAN CONVENTION.

The noble Lord alluded to the Amir's assent to the Anglo-Russian Convention. I heard his language on that point with the greatest regret. The Viceroy wrote to the Amir on the 10th September of last year, and on the 20th September the Amir replied that he was away on tour, but he would be back in November, and hoped then to consider the question. Since then he has not replied. Of course we only hear indirectly of proceedings in Kabul. The Amir has his Durbar to consider, and I suppose that in a Durbar, as in any other assembly, different points of view present themselves, and there are debates. Oriental debates, carried on without the assistance of guillotine or closure, are probably more prolonged than our own. The noble Lord said he did not wonder that the Amir feels no enthusiasm about the Convention. He used words implying that there are doubtful things in the interests of the Amir in this Convention. These words are sure to reach Kabul. What is the noble Lord doing? He is actually leading the Amir to think that, at the moment when we are on the eve of putting some pressure on him, there are those in England and in Parliament who do not at all wonder at his want of enthusiasm. Any one who realises what a proceeding of that kind in this Chamber means must feel that the noble Lord has not shown a considerate spirit in relation to delicate negotiations, not only as to Eastern things, but as to some very important European things.

THE VICEROY AND REFORM.

The noble Lord went into a very elaborate, careful, acute, and thoroughly experienced analysis of the causes of unrest. I think I am able to accept and to follow him into almost the whole of those causes. I think his diagnosis about education, about the tremendous influence of Japanese victories, and the other elements which he mentioned is thoroughly sound; but he did not say a word, and I admit it was not his business to say a word, about the course which he would advise His Majesty's Government or the Government of India to pursue. Of course, one policy is very simple. It can be expressed in the pithy formula which I heard the other day—if I may be forgiven for using a profane expression—"Martial law and no damned nonsense." Martial law and no nonsensical constitutional or other reforms—that is not the noble Lord's policy. I am perfectly sure; but I observe that everything that falls from him leads to the assumption that we must know and decide for ourselves, without overmuch reference to Indian demands and expectations, what form of so-called concessions we think fit to give them. I think the Viceroy himself was better inspired. I cannot sufficiently admire the manful courage in India with which, without yielding to panic or exaggeration on one side or to disgust at their blind, reckless, aimless crimes on the other, the Viceroy is ever persisting in the path which he and we have marked out for ourselves. *(Cheers.)* I think we can all realise the position of the Viceroy, surrounded as he is by influences of an alarmist kind. Lord Minto was appointed, not by my political friends, but by the Government of noble Lords opposite, and I can only say here, as I have said in another House, that between no two servants of the Crown is there a better understanding and a fuller confidence than there is between the present Viceroy and the present Secretary of State. *(Cheers.)* I admire the manful courage with which, in the very speech in which he was bringing in his Explosives Act and his Press Act, Lord Minto said:—"No anarchical crime will deter me from endeavouring to meet, as best I can, the political aspirations of honest reformers." I think that is a very fine utterance—fine in itself and fine considering the occasion. We have no choice but to persevere in the path of reform. We cannot get out of our own history. We cannot leave the course marked out for us by the conscience of this country in dealing with what I am sorry to call alien races.

In these days we cannot leave that out. I, for my part, accept the maxim of the French statesman, who said, "In politics you ought to take nothing tragically, everything seriously." The House will not be surprised if I say that nobody in it views more seriously than I do the crisis—I do not believe that is too strong a word—by which we are now confronted. We can only surmount its dangers and difficulties by looking calmly and composedly, that is, not to say without energy and force, at the problem which confronts us. We may postpone, but the longer you postpone, the greater will be the ulterior difficulties. I would be particularly glad if your Lordships will take this from me, that it is not merely Congressmen, it is not mere Moderates or Extremists in Indian parties. I read some Anglo-Indian newspapers, and find there, not as violently certainly, but just as sincerely, the expectation and hope for improvements in government and administration as I find in the Press of a more angry complexion. I believe from all the evidence that reaches me—I do not work these things out in my own head—from the members of the Indian Civil Service whom I have the pleasure of seeing from time to time that the Civil Service itself, the administrators great and small, will be as glad for an improvement and are looking as anxiously for an improvement in administration as the ordinary politician. Therefore, if we were to take our hands from the plough now, I do not say to adhere to every word in the scheme which the noble Lord has criticised, because of bombs and operations of that species, we should be exposed not only to the fury, the blind fury if you please so to call it, of the Extremists, not only to the lamentations of the Moderates, but we should be disappointing a great mass of strong Anglo-Indian, European opinion.

THE HOBHOUSE COMMISSION AND REFORMS.

The noble Lord said nothing about what is called the Hobhouse Commission. It was a Royal Commission which we appointed a few months ago with a view to examining what improvements in administration were possible, and I believe that when that Commission reports two or three months hence a great mass of valuable indication of the defects in the working of the Indian Government will be brought to light and suggestions of a fruitful kind made for their removal. There have been some complaints of excess of zeal in the Commission. That was inevitable, but I am confident that, when we get the report of that Commission, when we get back from India the scheme of reform mentioned by the noble Lord, with the opinion of local Governments of that scheme, we shall have before us a body of material not for the reconstruction of Indian Government—I, for my part, have no such ambition—but for taking steps which shall do two or three very important or even momentous things. One is administrative improvement, simplifying correspondence and appeals, and so on, simplifying the mass of writing which, as the noble Lord knows, is one of the curses of Indian procedure. Secondly, we shall, I hope, and, I feel confident, do something to give the Indian population in all their grades some formal and authorised opportunity of handling some of their own affairs. As at present advised, and subject to further consideration, I would hope they will be not only advisory, but though perhaps modest, executive powers. I will not detain the House any longer with a further exposition of what is at present incohate and without final and definite shape. There will, I hope, be something to limit excessive official interference; something, I hope, to stimulate the formation of independent opinions in local Governments and in district Governments. Whether or not the scheme, which, I trust, we shall be able to frame in concert with the Council of India and in constant communication with and reference to the Viceroy of India, will necessitate legislation and a direct appeal to Parliament—the scheme is not in a shape to enable me to answer that question—of course it would be idle to pretend to frame any scheme for which we did not expect to get full approval of Parliamentary opinion. I do not despair of that, and the noble Lord promised, as far as he was concerned, that there would be no particular criticism of measures of that kind, though he and his friends would, as they are bound to, look very closely into policy.

JUSTICE OF THE BRITISH PARLIAMENT.

Then there is the Indian party, or parties. They will make a great mistake if they give up the hope which they have hitherto always professed in the justice and good faith of this Parliament. I have heard that a friend of mine gruffly said to one of those who were talking of their faith in Parliament still remaining, in spite of a Secretary of State who, as the noble Lord said, has greatly disappointed them by his falling away from his earlier compositions. "You are worshipping a blind and deaf divinity." I do not agree. I do not believe that Parliament wishes either to be blind or deaf to any reasonable demands from India, provided those demands are made and pressed in a reasonable way and are kept clear of madness and of wicked crimes; and if they are backed by the responsible Executive Government, I have no fear of those demands not being complied with. One or two matters I have left out because I do not want to detain your Lordships. There was a certain passage between the noble Lord and Lord Middleton. In that passage I was *tertius gaudens*. I was sorry for it, because, if I may say so without impertinence, it is of great importance in the face of India that those leading public men who take part in Indian discussions should abstain, as far as they possibly can, whether, in despatches or otherwise, from anything calculated to make the people believe that we look for a moment to any personal considerations of one kind or another in view of the tremendous issues by which we are confronted. I thank your Lordships for your consideration. (*Cheers.*)

SPEECH
AT THE CIVIL SERVICE DINNER.

[*The following speech was delivered by Viscount Morley of Blackburn at the Civil Service Dinner held in London, July,* 1908 :—]

GENTLEMEN :—I have first of all to thank you for what I understand is the rare honour—and an honour it assuredly is—of being invited to be your guest to-night. The position of a Secretary of State in the presence of the Indian Civil Service is not an entirely simple one. You, Gentlemen, who are still in the Service, and the veterans I see around me who have been in that great Service, naturally and properly look first of all, and almost altogether, upon India. A Secretary of State has to look also upon Great Britain and upon Parliament—and it is not always a perfectly easy situation to adjust. I forget who it was who said about the rulers of India in India :—"It is no easy thing for a man to keep his watch on two longitudes at once at the same time." That is the case of the Secretary of State. It is not the business of the Secretary of State to look exclusively at India, though I will confess to you for myself that during the moderately short time I have held my present office I have kept my eye upon India constantly, steadfastly, and with every desire to learn the whole truth upon every situation as it arose. But Janus is a deity for whom upon the whole of all the old deities I have the least respect.

But what I regard as a cardinal rule in Indian administration from the point of view of the India Office is, that there shall be a thorough comprehension in the mind of the Secretary of State of two things—first of all, of the Indian point of view; and, secondly, the point of view as it appears to those who are the masters of me and of you. Do not forget that adjustment has to be made, and, though the times during my two-and-a-half years of office have not been altogether plain sailing—so far that adjustment has been rather effectually made. I will say more, gentlemen—that whether it be myself, though I have some advantages from party position—whether it be myself, or whether it be some successor of me from another party—have we another party? (*A voice, "No,"*)—However that may be, somehow or other—and I say this to all whom it concerns—the voice and the will of the people of this island will be on the whole a unanimous voice. Now it really would be impertinent of me to pay compliments to the Civil Service, to whom I propose this toast—"The Health of the Indian Civil Service." You might think for a moment that it was an amateur proposing prosperity and success to experts. I have had in my days a good deal to do with experts of one kind or another, and I assure you that I do not think an expert is a bit the worse when he gets a candid-minded and well trained amateur.

Now, this year is a memorable anniversary. It is fifty years within a month or two, I think, since the Crown took over the Government of India from the old East India company. Whether that was a good move or a bad move it would not become me to discuss. The move was made. (*A voice, "It was a good move."*) My veteran friend says that it was a good move. I hope so. But at the end of fifty years we are in rather a critical moment. I read in the *Times* the other day that the present Viceroy and Secretary of State had to deal with conditions such as the British in India never before were called upon to face. (*A voice, "That is so."*) Now, many of you sitting around me at this table are far better able to test the weight of that statement than I can pretend to be. It is true that at the end of fifty years of the transfer to the Crown we have to deal with conditions such as the British in India never before were called upon to face? (*"Yes."*) I cannot undertake to measure that; but what is clear is that rather heavy clouds have suddenly risen in our horizon, and that those rather heavy clouds are now sailling over our Indian skies. That cannot be denied. But, gentlemen, having paid the utmost attention that a man can, in office, with access to all the papers, and seeing all the observers he is able to see, I do not feel for a moment that this discovery of a secret society or a secret organisation involves any question of an earthquake. I prefer to look upon it, to revert to my own figure, as clouds sailing through the sky. I do not say you will not have to take pretty strong measures of one sort and another. Yes, but strong measures in the right direction, and with the right qualifications, if you want to get that bank of cloud dispersed. It may prove to be more. I think any man who lays down a firm proposition that all is well, or any man who says that all is ill—that either of those two men is probably wrong. Now this room is filled and joyfully filled, with men who have had enormous experience, vast and wide experience, over, I am sorry to think, for some of them, a good many years. It is filled with men of wide experience, and, not merely of passive experience, but of that splendid active experience which is the real training and education of men in responsibility. This room is full of gentlemen with these qualifications. And I will venture to say that the theories and explanations which could be heard in the palace of truth from all of you gentlemen here, would be countless in their differences. I hear explanations of the present state of things all day long. I like to hear them. You think it may become monotonous. No: I think not, because there is so much, I will not say of random variety, but there is so much independent use of mind upon the facts that we have to deal with, that I, for one, am delighted to hear these various views. But, I think, and I wish I could think otherwise with all my heart—and you will all feel the same—that to sum up all these theories and explanations of the state of things with which we have to deal, and you have the rather painful fact that there is now a certain estrangement and alienation of races in India. ("*No, No.*") Gentlemen, bear with me patiently.

THE UNWISDOM OF REPRESSION.

I am trying to feel my way through the most difficult problem, the most difficult situation that I think responsible Governments, you and I, and all of us, ever had to face. Of course, I am dependent upon information. But as I read it, as I listen to great Indian experts with large experience, there is a certain view like, I hope it is so, superficial estrangement and alienation. Now that is the problem that we have to deal with. Gentlemen, I should very badly repay your kindness in asking me to come among you to-night if I were to attempt for a minute to analyse or to prove all the conditions that have led to this state of things. It would need hours and hours. This is not, I think, the occasion for that, nor is it the moment for it. Our first duty—the first duty of any Government—is to keep order. But first remember this. It would be idle to deny, and I am not sure that any of you gentlemen would deny, that there is at this moment, and there has been for some little time past, and very likely there will be for some time to come, a living movement in the mind of those people for whom you are responsible. A living movement, and a movement for what? A movement for objects which we ourselves have all taught them to think desirable objects. And unless we somehow or other can reconcile order with satisfaction of those ideas and aspirations, gentlemen, the fault will not be theirs. It will be ours. It will mark the breakdown of what has never yet broken down in any part of the world—the breakdown of British statesmanship. That is what it will do. Now nobody, I think—I do not believe anybody either in this room or out of this room—believes that we can now enter upon an era of pure repression. You cannot enter at this date and with English public opinion, mind you, watching you, upon an era of pure repression and I do not believe really that anybody desires any such thing. I do not believe so. Gentlemen, we have seen attempts, in the lifetime of some of us here tonight, we have seen attempts, in Continental Europe, to govern by pure repression, and indeed, in days not altogether remote from our own, we have seen attempts of that sort. They have all failed. There may be now and again a spurious semblance of success, but in truth they have all failed. Whether we with our enormous power and resolution should fail, I do not know. But I do not believe anybody in this room representing so powerfully as it does dominant sentiments which are not always felt in England—that in this room there is anybody who is for an era of pure repression. Gentlemen, I would just divert for a moment if I am not tiring you. ("*Go, on.*") About the same time as the transfer, about fifty years ago, of the Government of India from the old East India Company to the Crown another very important step was taken, a step which I have often thought since I have been concerned with the Government of India was far more momentous one far deeper than the mere mechanical transfer, so to call it, to the Crown. And what do you think that was? That was the first establishment—I think I am right in my date—of Universities. We in this country are so accustomed to look upon political changes as the important changes that we very often forget—sometimes we think of fiscal changes—that there was a change in the establishment of Universities. And if any of you are inclined to prophesy, I should like to read to you something that was written by that great and famous man Lord Macaulay—yes, indeed, a great and famous man—in the year 1836, long before the Universities were thought of. What did he say? What a warning it is, gentlemen, He wrote, in the year 1836:—

> At the single town of Hooghly 1,400 boys are learning English. The effect of this education on the Hindus is prodigious..........It is my firm belief that if our plans of education are followed up, there will not be a single idolater among the respectable classes in Bengal thirty years hence. And this will be effected merely by the natural operation of knowledge and reflection.

Ah, gentlemen, the natural operation of knowledge and reflection carries men of a different structure of mind, different beliefs, different habits and customs of life—it carries them into strange and unexpected paths. I am not going to embark you to-night upon these great controversies, but I for my own part, speaking without arrogance, without arrogant presumption, feel when we talk about education that we are getting very near the root of the case. Now to-night we are not in the humour—I am sure you are not, I certainly am not—for philosophising. Somebody is glad of it. I will tell you what I think of—as I have for a good many days past—I think of the burden of responsibility weighing on the governing man at Calcutta and at Simla.

ATTITUDE OF EUROPEANS IN INDIA.

We think—you do too—of the anxieties of those in India, and in England as well, who have relatives in remote places and under conditions that are very familiar to you all. I have a great admiration for the self-command, for the freedom from anything like panic, which has hitherto marked the attitude of the European population of Calcutta and some other places, and I confess I have said to myself that if they had found here, in London, bombs in the railway carriages, bombs under the Prime Minister's House, and so forth, we should have had tremendous scare headlines and all the other phenomena of excitement and panic. So far as I am informed, though very serious in Calcutta—the feeling is serious, how could it be anything else?—they have exercised that great and noble virtue in all ranks and classes of self-command. Now the Government—if you will allow me for a very few moments to say a word on behalf of the Government, not here alone but at Simla—we and they, for after all we are one—have been assailed for a certain want of courage and what is called, often grossly miscalled, vigour.

THE COURAGE OF THE GOVERNMENT.

We were told the other day—and this brings us to the root of policy—that there had been a momentary flash of courage when the Government of India and we here assented to the deportation of two men, and it is made a matter of complaint that they were released immediately. Well, they were not released immediately, but after six or eight months—I forget exactly how many months—of detention. They were there with no charge. You are in England now, gentlemen. There was no charge, no trial, nor intention of bringing them to trial. How long were we to keep them there? I will tell *you*—and I say it in the presence of all concerned in this business or in this accusation (I will not say accusation, but hint) that we have been wanting in courage—how long were we to keep those men there? Not a day, I answer, nor one hour after this specific and particular mischief, with a view to which this drastic proceeding was adopted, had abated. Specific mischief, mind you. I will not go into that argument to-night: another day I will. I will only say one thing. To strain the meaning and the spirit of an exceptional law like our old regulation of the year 1818 in such a fashion as this, what would it do? I will tell you with my full responsibility, with my most careful reading of the history of our own day and of some other days. Such a strain of the law as this, in the perverse imagination of headstrong men, a suggestion for provoking lawless and criminal reprisals. ("No.") You may not agree with me. You are kindly allowing me as your guest to say things with which perhaps you do not agree. (*Cries of "Go on."*) Though you are the Indian

Civil Service and I am Secretary of State, we understand one another—we speak the same language, and I tell you that a proceeding of that kind, indefinite detention, is a thing which would not be endured in this country. (*A voice of "Disorder."*) Yes, if there were great and clear connection between the detention and the outbreak of disorder, certainly; but as the disorder had abated it would have been intolerable for us to continue that incarceration.

THE PRESS LAW.

Last Monday, what is called a Press Act, was passed by the Government of India in connection with and simultaneously with an Explosives Act which ought to have been passed, I should think, twenty years ago. What is the purport of the Press Act? That is what I ask your kind attention to, and the kind attention of a few people outside this room. I do not attempt to give it in technical language. Where the Local Government finds a newspaper article inciting to murder and violence, or resort to explosives for the purposes of murder or violence, that Local Government may apply to a Magistrate of a certain status to issue an order for the seizure of the Press by which that incitement has been printed; and if the owner of the Press feels himself aggrieved, he may within fifteen days ask the High Court to reverse the order and direct the restoration of the Press. (*Cries of "Oh."*) That is a statement of the law which has been passed in India, and to which I do not doubt we shall give our assent. There has been the usual outcry raised—usual in all these cases; I am not unfamiliar with it in another connection—between "too early" on the one hand and "too late" on the other. Certain people say: "Oh, you are too late." Others say: "You are too early." I will say to you first of all, and to any other audience afterwards, that I have no apology to make for being a party to the passing of this law now; and I have no apology to make for not passing it before. I do not believe in short cuts, and I believe that the Government in these difficult circumstances is wise not to be in too great a hurry. I have no apology to make for introducing executive action into what would normally be a judicial process. Neither, on the other hand, have I any apology to make for tempering executive action with judicial elements; and I am very glad to say that an evening newspaper last night, which is not of the politics to which I belong, entirely approves of that. It says: "You must show that you are not afraid of referring your semi-executive, semi-judicial action to the High Court." You will all argue about that. But I want to say—thinking more of others than of you—that this Act meddles with no criticism, however strong, of Government measures. It discourages the advocacy of no policy, social, moral, political, or economic. Yet I see, to my great regret and astonishment, that this Act is described—and, I am sorry to say in an organ of my own party—as an Act for judging cases of seditious libel without a Jury. It is contended by some—and I respect the contention—

that the Imperial Parliament ought to have been consulted before this Act was passed, and ought to be consulted now (*Cries of "No, no."*) My veteran friends lived before the days of household suffrage. But it is said, and I think quite rightly,—that the voice of Parliament ought to be heard in so grave a matter as this. But the principles of the proposals were fully considered, as was quite right, not only by the Secretary of State in Council, but by the Cabinet. It was a matter of Police urgency. That is my view of it. Do not think I am trying to find pleas to excuse this Act. Not a bit of it. I stand by it. But it is perfectly natural to say: Should the Imperial Parliament have no voice? I have directed the Government of India to report to the Secretary of State all the proceedings taken under this Act; and I undertake, as long as I hold the office of Secretary of State, to present to Parliament from time to time the reports of the proceedings taken under this somewhat drastic Act. I do not believe that any of you will feel that this is at all a weakening of our determination to carry out this Act.

THE FREEDOM OF THE PRESS.

When I am told that an Act of this kind is a restriction on the freedom of the Press, I do not accept it for a moment. I do not believe that there is a man in England who is more jealous of the freedom of the Press than I am. But let us see what we mean. It is said: "Oh, these incendiary articles"—for they are incendiary and murderous—"are mere froth."

Yes, they are froth; but they are froth stained with bloodshed. When you have men admitting that they deliberately write these articles and promote these newspapers with a view of furthering murderous action, to talk of the freedom of the Press in connection with that is wicked moonshine. We have now got a very Radical House of Commons. So much the better for you. If I were still a member of the House of Commons, I should not mind for a moment going down to the House—and I am sure that my colleagues will not mind—to say that when you find these articles on the avowal of those concerned, expressly designed to promote murderous action and when you find as a fact that murderous action has come about, it is moonshine to talk of the freedom of the Press. There is no good in indulging in heroics. They are not wanted. But an incendiary article is part and parcel of the murderous act. You may put picric acid in the ink and pen just as much as in any steel bomb. I have one or two extracts here with which I will not trouble you. But when I am told that we may recognise it as one of the chief aims of good Government that there may be as much public discussion as possible, I read that sentence with great edification; and then I turn to what I had telegraphed far from India—extracts from *Yugantar*. To talk of public discussion in connection with things of that kind is really pushing things too far.

PUBLIC OPINION.

I will not be in a hurry to believe that there is

not a great body in India of reasonable people, not only among the quiet, humble, law-abiding people, but among the educated classes. I will not believe that there is not a great body of reasonable people of that kind. I do not care what they call themselves, or what organisation they may form themselves into. But I will not be in a hurry to believe that there are no such people and that we cannot depend on them. When we believe that—that we have no body of organised, reasonable people on our side in India—when you gentlemen who know the country say that—and, mind you, you must have that body of opinion among the educated classes as well as among the great masses, because it is the educated classes in all countries and in all times who make all the difference—I say that, on the day that we believe that, we shall be confronted with as awkward, as embarrassing, and as hazardous a situation as has ever confronted the rulers of the most complex and gigantic state in human history. I am confident that if the crisis comes it will find us ready, but let us keep our minds clear now. There have been many dark and ugly moments—I see gentlemen around me who have gone through dark and ugly moments—in our relations with India before now. We have such a dark and ugly moment before us and we shall get through it—but only with self-command and without any quackery or cant, whether it be the quackery and cant of order or the quackery and cant of sentiment. I beg to propose the health of the Indian Civil Service.

THE REFORM PROPOSALS.

[*The following is the full text of the speech delivered by Lord Morley in the House of Lords on the 17th December, 1908, in introducing the Reform Proposals* :—]

I feel that some apology is due to the House for the delay of which I have been the innocent cause. It has been said that my delay in bringing forward this subject is due to my anxiety to burke discussion. That is not in the least true. The reasons which seemed to me to make it desirable that discussion upon this most important and far-reaching range of topics should be postponed are reasons of common sense. In the first place, discussion without any one having seen the papers to be discussed would be ineffective; second, it would be impossible to discuss these papers without knowing, at all events to some degree, the nature of their reception in the country immediately concerned: and, third, I cannot but apprehend that discussion in Parliament would be calculated to prejudice the reception in India of the proposals which the Government of India and the Government at Home have agreed to make. This afternoon your Lordships will be presented with a modest volume of one hundred pages, but to-morrow morning there will be ready a series of papers so numerous that the most voracious appetite for Blue-Books will have ample food for the Christmas holidays. (*Laughter.*)

AN IMPORTANT EPOCH.

This is the opening of a very important chapter in the history of the relations between Great Britain and India. I suppose, like other Secretaries of State for India, I found my first idea was to have what they used to have in the old days—a permanent Committee to inquire into Indian Government. On the whole, I think there is a great deal in the present day to be said against that idea. Therefore, what I have done at the instigation of the Government of India is to open a chapter of constitutional reform of which I will speak in a moment; and, in the next place, I appointed a Royal Commission to enquire into the internal relations between the Government of India and its subordinate and co-ordinate departments. That Commission will, I hope, report in February or March of next year, and that again will involve both the Government of India and the India Office in laborious and careful inquiries. Unfortunately the delay which has taken place has not made the skies any brighter. But do not let us make the sky cloudier than it really is; do not let us consider the clouds darker than they really are. Let us look at the formidable difficulties which confront us without any undue sense of apprehension, and I can give no better example of what I mean than what I may call the intrepid coolness of Lord Minto. (*Cheers.*)

What is the state of things as they appear to persons of authority and ample knowledge in India? Well, the anarchists are few, but, on the other hand, they are apparently prepared to go any length and run any risk. An Indian friend of mine informs me that there is no fear of anything in the nature of a rising, but that if murders continue a general panic may arise and greatly increase the danger of the situation. We cannot hope that any machinery will completely stop the outrages at once, but there is a growing indication that the native population itself is alarmed, and that the Government of India will have strong support from native public opinion. In substance, the view of the Government in India is that the position of our Government in India is as sound and well-founded as it has ever been. (*Cheers.*)

THE ANTI-ANARCHIST LEGISLATION.

Then why, it may be asked, have the Government of India found it necessary to pass measures introducing drastic machinery? I share full responsibility for those measures. Quite early after coming to the India office I had pressure put upon me to repeal the regulations of 1818, under which natives are now being deported without trial, without charges, or without intention to try or charge. That, of course, is a tremendous power to place in the hands of an Executive Government, but I declined to take out of the hands of the Government of India any weapon they possessed in circumstances so obscure, so formidable, and so impenetrable as the circumstances surrounding British Government in India. There are two paths of folly. One is to regard Indian matters as if they had to do with Great Britain or Ireland, and to insist that all powers must necessarily suit India; and the other is that all we have to do is, as to my amazement I have seen suggested in print, to blow a certain number of men from guns.

I do not ignore the frightful risks involved in transferring what ought to be power under the law into the power of arbitrary personal discretion. I do not forget the tremendous price we pay for all operations of this sort in the reaction and excitement which they provoke. But there are situations in which a responsible Government is bound to run these risks and pay this possible price. It is like war—a hateful thing. The only question for us is whether there is such a situation in India to-day as to justify the passing of this Act of the other day, and to justify a resort to 1818. I cannot imagine that any one reading the list of crimes given the other day, and remembering all that they stand for, can have any doubt that summary procedure is justified and called for.

After all, it is not our fault that India is like what it is. We must protect the peaceful inhabitants, both Indian and European, from bloodshed. Believe me, it is no matter of form when I say—and I believe every-body in this House would say the same thing—that I deplore this necessity; but we are bound to face the fact, and I myself, recognise the necessity with infinite regret, and something much deeper than regret. But it is not Government here or in India who are the authors of this necessity, and I would not at all mind, if it were not impertinent or unbecoming on my part, to stand up in another place and say there what I say here—that I will do my best to support the Government. (*Cheers.*)

Now, the first important question that arises is that of reform, and I would ask your Lordships to give close attention to it for a moment, because I am sure that here and elsewhere it will be argued that the necessity and the facts that cause strong repressive measures should arrest our policy of reforms. That has already been stated, and many people agree. But the Government of India and myself have, from the beginning never varied in our determination to persevere in our policy of reform. (*Cheers.*) Perseverance in our plan of reform is not a concession to violence. Reforms we have publicly adopted and worked out for more than two years. It is no concession now too to violence to proceed with those reforms. It is simply standing to our guns, and is no weakness.

A gentleman to whom I would refer with the greatest respect recently addressed me in the public Press exhorting me to remember that Oriental countries invariably interpret kindness into fear. When I am told that Orientals always mistake kindness for fear, I can only say I do not believe a word of it, any more than I believe the strong saying of Carlyle that, after all, the fundamental question between two human beings is "Can I kill thee, or canst thou kill me?" (*Laughter.*) I do not believe that either Oriental or Western society ever existed on either of these terms or that brutality is a true test of the relations between men. There are two alternative courses open to us. We must either withdraw our reforms or persevere with them. The first would be a most flagrant sign of weakness. The second alternative is to hold steadily on in spite of bombs. That is the point. Are we to let ourselves be openly forced by bombs or murder clubs to drop our policy? Who are those who would be best pleased if I were to allow your Lordships to-night to sanction that the Government should drop these reforms? It is notorious that the men best pleased would be the extremists, the irreconcilables (*cheers*), because they know that if we do anything to soften the estrangement or appease the European or native population it would be the best way of driving them from their sinister and mischievous designs.

THE NEED FOR REFORMS.

Therefore, I hope you will agree that we are not wrong in proceeding with these reforms. Sir Norman Baker, the new Lieutenant-Governor of Bengal, declared that, if these powers were not enough, he would apply for more, but he also said that these measures did not represent even a major part of the policy of dealing with the situation, and he believed that, when the constitutional reforms were finally announced, the task of restoring order in India would be on the road to accomplishment. For a man in Sir Norman's position to make a statement like that is sufficient, and all that Lord Minto needs, is to ask His Majesty's Government to proceed with the reforms. Experienced men, officials and others to whom I have put the question have replied that to withdraw is impossible. We cannot stand still. Supposing we did, I would not be surprised if there are not gentleman here who would say that we ought to take some strong measures for putting down the free Press. A long time ago Sir Thomas Munro used the language which I will quote in order that all who hear me, and all who read, may feel what tremendous difficulties arise—difficulties which our successors, as our predecessors, will encounter. Sir Thomas Munro said:—

> What we are trying to do is an experience never yet tried in the world—that of maintaing a foreign dominion by means of a native army, and teaching that army, through a native Press that they ought to expel us and deliver their country.

And he went on to say that a tremendous revolution might take place in consequence of a free Press. I recognise to the full the enormous force in a declaration of that kind; but let us look at it as practical men who govern the country. Supposing you abolish freedom of the Press, that will not do your business. You will then have to shut up the schools and colleges, because it would be no use abolishing the papers if you did not close these. But that will not do it. You will have to stop the printing of unlicensed books, and you will have to have repressive book legislation, as you have repressive regulations for bombs. But supposing you had done all this. When you had made India blind and gagged her, would you be able to call India, as now, the brightest jewel in the Imperial

Crown? No, you could not. The last man to minimise such a policy is the present Governor-General of India, the despatches between whom and the Government will be in your Lordship's hands to-morrow.

THE PLAN OF REFORMS.

But what of the plan of reforms. I think you will find that we have been guided in our policy by an expansion of the principles that were recognised so far back as 1861, and by the noble Marquess opposite in 1892. In 1892, the noble Marquess (the Marquess of Landsdowne) said he hoped we—meaning the Government of the day—had succeeded in giving to our proposals of Legislative Council reform sufficient to secure a satisfactory advance in the representation of the people on the Council and to give effect to the principle of selection, as far as possible, to such sections of the community as might be capable of assisting us in that manner. The noble Marquess (the Marquess of Ripon)—whom I am pleased to see here to-night—in 1882 said that the measure then put forward was chiefly designed as an instrument of political principle and popular education. Those are the doctrines announced by the noble Marquess opposite and by my noble friend behind, and that is the point of view from which we approached the position.

I believe that the House will be satisfied—as I confess I am—with the amount of patience which has been bestowed upon the preparation of the scheme in India, and I hope I may add that it has been treated with equal patience and candour here with us. The result is that although some points of difficulty arose, and though the Government of India decided to drop certain parts of the scheme, on the whole there has been complete and remarkable agreement between the Government of India and myself as to the best way of dealing with these proceedings in the Legislative Council.

What you are to consider to-day will open up a great chapter in the history of India. This is the list of powers we shall have to take from Parliament when we bring in this Bill, which I propose to do next year:—

1. At present the maximum and minimum number of the Legislative Council is fixed by Statute, and we shall come to Parliament to authorise an increase in the number both of the Viceregal and the Provincial Councils.

2. Members are now nominated by the Viceroy or the Governor or the Lieutenant-Governor. No election takes place in the strict sense of the word. The nearest approach is nomination by the Viceroy on recommendation by a majority of voters, on certain public bodies. We do not propose to ask Parliament to abolish nomination but we ask them to sanction election alongside of nomination, with a view to having due representation of the different classes of the country.

3. The Indian Councils Act of 1892 forbids either Resolution or division in Council in financial discussions, and we shall ask Parliament to repeal this prohibition.

4. We shall propose to invest Legislative Councils with power to discuss matters of public and general importance, and to pass recommendations to the Government.

5. We propose to extend the power that at present exists to appoint a Member on the Council to preside.

6. Bombay and Madras have Executive Councils and I propose to ask Parliament for power to double the number.

7. The Lieutenant-Governor has no Executive Council, and we shall ask Parliamentary sanction for the creation of such a Council, not exceeding two, and to define the Lieutenant-Governor's power to over-rule his Council.

THE OFFICIAL MAJORITY.

I now come to a very important point on which there may be differences of opinion, and which will, no doubt, create some controversy; I mean the official majority on the Provincial Legislative Councils. It may be said that these Councils, if you take away the safeguard of an official majority, will pass all manner of wild-cat Bills. The answer to that is that the Governor-General can withhold his assent. That is not a defunct authority, but a living power, and has been used with the happiest results by the Governor-General in the case of a legislative mistake in a local Legislative Council since I have been in office. It should be remembered, when thinking of wild-eat Bills, that the range of subjects within the sphere of Provincial Legislature is rigorously limited by Statutory exclusions, though more than one subject of first importance still remains. There is one proviso in the matter of the provincial majority which may, perhaps, be regarded as a surprise. I do not propose to dispense with the official majority in the Viceroy's Legislative Council. We lag behind a stage in this respect, for you will find the Government of India saying :—

> On all ordinary occasions we are ready to dispense with an official majority in the Imperial Legislative Council, and to rely on the public spirit of non-official members to enable us to carry on the ordinary work of legislation.

If I were endeavouring to set up a Parliamentary system in India, it would be the easiest thing in the world to convict me of bad logic for not dropping the necessity of an official majority in the Central as in the Provincial Councils. If it could be said that what I propose would lead directly up to the establishment of Parliamentary system in India, I, for one, would have nothing at all to do with it. I do not believe it will, in spite of the attempts in Oriental countries at this moment—attempts which we all wish well—to set up Parliamentary Government. It is no ambition of mine to have any share in the beginning of that operation. (*Cheers.*) If I know that my days, either official or corporeal, were twenty times longer than they are likely to be, I should be sorry to set out for the goal of a Parliamentary system in India. The Parliamentary system in India is not the goal to which I for one moment aspire.

THE VICEROY'S EXECUTIVE COUNCIL.

I now turn to the question of a native Member on the Viceroy's Executive Council. The absence of a native Member from that Council can no longer be defended. There is nothing to prevent the Secretary of State recommending His Majesty to appoint an Indian member to fill any vacancy, and I want to say that, if, during my retention of office, there should be a vacancy in the Viceroy's Executive Council, I should feel it my duty to tender to the King my advice that an Indian member should be appointed. I would not do it on my own authority only. I am not fond of treading on dark and obscure ground, and here I have the absolute and full concurrence of Lord Minto himself. It was at Lord Minto's special instigation that I began to think seriously of it, and so this is how it stands: You have at this moment a Viceroy and a Secretary of State who both concur in a recommendation of this kind.

If I may be allowed to give a personal turn to these matters, I may say that I suppose Lord Minto and I have had very different experiences of life and the world, and we belong to different schools of national politics. It is rather a remarkable thing that two men differing in this way—in antecedents and so forth—should concur in this proposal. The object of it is to show that the merits of individuals are to be considered irrespective of race and colour. We need not now discuss what particular portfolio should be assigned. That will be settled by the Viceroy on the merits of the individual. A year ago I appointed two Indian gentlemen to be Members of the Secretary of State's Council, and many apprehensions reached me as to what might happen. So far those apprehensions have all been dissipated. The concord between the two Indian Members of the Council and their colleagues has been perfect; their work has been good; and the advantage to me to be able to talk with one or other of these two gentlemen, and so realise the Indian point of view, has been enormous. I actually feel sometimes as though I have been transported to the streets of Calcutta. Is it not common sense? Everybody in India recognises the advantages derived from the admission of Indians to the Bench of the High Court with their intimate knowledge of the country and the conditions of the lives of the people. I propose at once, if Parliament agrees, to acquire powers to double the Executive Councils in Bombay and Madras, and to appoint at least one Indian member in each case. Nor shall I be backward in advancing towards similar steps as occasion may require in respect to at least four of the major provinces.

GLOOMY VIEWS UNNECESSARY.

I wish it had fallen that this chapter had been opened at a more fortunate moment, but I repeat what I said when I rose—do not let us for a moment take a gloomy view of the situation. There is not the slightest occasion for it, and none of those who are responsible take a gloomy view. We know the difficulties, and are prepared to grapple with them and keep down mutinous opposition ; and we hope to attract the good-will which must, after all, be the real foundation of the prosperity and strength in India. We believe that this is so far unsapped, and we believe that the admission of Indians to a more responsible share in the Government of their country, without for a moment taking from the central power its authority, will strengthen the foundations of our position. It will require great steadiness and constant pursuit of the same objects, with the assistance, under responsible circumstances, of Indians themselves. Military strength and material strength we have in abundance. What we still want to acquire is moral strength in guiding and controlling the people of India in the course on which time has launched them. I should like to read a few words from a speech delivered by Mr. Bright in 1858, when the Government of India Bill was in another place. What he said was this:—

> We do not know how to leave it, and therefore let us see if we know how to govern it. Let us abandon all that system of calumny against the natives of India which has lately prevailed. Had that people not been docile, the most governable race in the world, how could you have maintained your power for 100 years? Are they not industrious, are they not intelligent, are they not, upon the evidence of the most distinguished men the Indian Service ever produced, endowed with many qualities which make them respected by all Englishmen who mix with them? I should not permit any man in my presence without rebuke to indulge in the calumnies and expressions of contempt which I have recently heard poured forth without measure upon the whole population of India. The people of India do not like us, but they would scarcely know where to turn if we left them. They are all sheep, literally without a shepherd.

However that may be, the Government have no choice and no option. As an illustrious member of this House, Lord Macaulay, wrote:—"We found a society in a state of decomposition, and we have undertaken the serious and stupendous process of reconstructing it." Lord Macaulay said: "India now is like Europe in the fifth century." A stupendous process indeed, but one which has gone on with marvellous success! And if we are all, according to our various lights, true to our colours, that process will go on. I am not what is commonly called an Imperialist, but so far from denying it, I most emphatically affirm that it is for us to preside over this transition from the fifth European century, in some parts, in slow stages up to the twentieth. It is for us to be the guides of people in that condition, and this duty, if conducted with humanity and sympathy and wisdom and political courage, is not only a human duty and a great national honour, but what it was called the other day—one of the most glorious tasks ever confided to any country.

SECOND READING OF THE INDIAN COUNCILS BILL.

[*The following is the full text of Lord Morley's speech in the House of Lords on February 23, 1909 :—*]

My Lords, I invite the House to take to-day the first definite and operative step in carrying out the policy that I had the honour of describing to your Lordships just before Christmas, and that has occupied the active consideration both of the Home Government and of the Government of India for very nearly three years. The statement was awaited in India with an expectancy that with time became impatience, and it was received in India—and that, after all, is the point to which I looked with the most anxiety—with intense interest and attention and various degree of approval, from warm enthusiasm to cool assent and acquiescence.

A few days after the arrival of my despatch, a deputation waited upon the Viceroy, unique in its comprehensive character. Both Hindus and Mahomedans were represented; and they waited upon the Viceroy to offer warm expressions of gratitude for the scheme that was unfolded before them. A few days later at Madras the Congress met; they, too, expressed their thanks to the Home Government and to the Government of India. The Moslem League met at Amritsar; they were warm in their approval of the policy which they took to be foreshadowed in the despatch, though they found fault with the defects they thought they had discovered in the scheme, and implored the Government, both in India and here, to remedy those defects. So far as I know—and I do beg your Lordships to note these details of the reception of our policy in India—there has been no sign in any quarter, save in the irreconcilable camp, of anything like organised, hostile opinion among either Indians or Anglo-Indians.

The Indian Civil Service I will speak of very shortly. I will pass them by for the moment. Lord Lansdowne said truly the other night that when spoke at the end of December, I used the words "formidable and obscure" as describing the situation, and he desired to know whether I thought the situation was still obscure and formidable. I will not abandon the words, but I think the situation is less formidable and less obscure. Neither repression on the one hand, nor reform on the other, could possibly be expected to cut the roots of anarchical crime in a few weeks. But with unfaltering repression on the one hand, and vigour and good faith in reform on the other, we see solid reason to hope that we shall weaken, even if we cannot destroy, those baneful forces.

There are, I take it, three classes of people that we have to consider in dealing with a scheme of this kind. There are the extremists, who nurse fantastic dreams that some day they will drive us out of India. In this group there are academic extremists and physical force extremists, and I have seen it stated on a certain authority—it cannot be more than a guess—that they do not number, whether academic or physical force extremists, more than one-tenth, or even three per cent., of what are called the educated class in India. The second group nourish no hopes of this sort; they hope for autonomy or self-government of the colonial species and pattern. The third section in this classification ask for no more than to be admitted to co-operation in our administration, and to find a free and effective voice in expressing the interests and needs of their people. I believe the effect of the reforms has been, is being, and will be, to draw the second class, who hope for colonial autonomy, into the ranks of the third class, who will be content with admission to a fair and workable co-operation. A correspondent wrote to me the other day and said:—

> We seem to have caught many discontented people on the rebound, and to have given them an excuse for a loyalty which they have badly wanted.

In spite of all this, it is a difficult and critical situation. Still, by almost universal admission it has lost the tension that strained India two or three months ago, and public feeling is tranquillised, certainly beyond any expectation that either I or the Viceroy ventured to entertain.

The atmosphere has changed from dark and sullen to hopeful, and I am sure your Lordships will allow me to be equally confident that nothing will be done at Westminster to overcloud that promising sky. The noble Marquess the other day said—and I was delighted to hear it—that he, at all events, would give us, with all the reservations that examination of the scheme might demand from him, a whole-hearted support here, and his best encouragement to the men in India. I accept that, and I lean upon it, because if anything were done at Westminster, either by delay or otherwise, to show a breach in what ought to be the substantial unity of Parliamentary opinion in face of the Indian situation, it would be a marked disaster. I would venture on the point of delay to say this. Your Lordships will not suspect me of having any desire to hurry the Bill, but I remember that when Lord Cross brought in the Bill of 1892, Lord Kimberley, so well-known and so popular in this House, used language which I venture to borrow from him, and to press upon your Lordships to-day:—

> I think it almost dangerous to leave a subject of this kind hung up to be perpetually discussed by all manner of persons, and, having once allowed that, at all events, some amendment is necessary in regard to the mode of constituting the Legislative Councils; it is incumbent upon the Government and Parliament to pass the Bill which they may think expedient as speedily as possible into law.

Considerations of social order and social urgency in India make that just as useful to be remembered to-day, as it was useful then.

The noble Marquess the other day, in a very courteous manner, administered to me an exhortation and an admonition—I had almost said a lecture—as to the propriety of deferring to the man on the spot, and the danger of quarrelling with the man on the spot. I listened with becoming meekness and humility, but then it occurred to me that the language of the noble

Marquess was not original. Those noble Lords who share the Bench with him, gave deep murmurs of approval to the homily that was administered to me. They forgot that they once had a man on the spot, the man then being that eminent and distinguished personage whom I may be allowed to congratulate upon his restoration to health and to his place in this Assembly. He said this, which the noble Marquess will see is a fair original for his own little discourse; it was said after the noble Lord had thrown up the reins:—

> What I wish to say to high officers of State and members of Government is this, as far as you can, trust the man on the spot. Do not weary or fret or nag him with your superior wisdom. They claim no immunity from errors of opinion or judgment, but their errors are nothing compared with yours.

The remonstrance, therefore, of Lord Curzon addressed to the noble Lords sitting near him, is identical, with the warning which I have laid to heart from the noble Marquess.

The House will pardon me if for a moment I dwell upon what by application is an innuendo conveyed in the admonition of the noble Marquess. I have a suspicion that he considered his advice was needed; he expressed the hope that all who were responsible for administration in India would have all the power for which they had a right to ask. Upon that I can—though I am half reluctant to do it—completely clear my character. In December last, shortly before I addressed your Lordships, Lord Minto, having observed there was some talk of my interference with him and his Council, telegraphed these words, and desired that I should make use of them whenever I thought fit:—

I hope you will say from me in as strong language as you may choose to use, that in all our dealings with sedition I could not be more strongly supported than I have been by you. The question of the control of Indian administration by the Secretary of State, mixed up as it is with the old difficulties of centralisation, we may very possibly look at from different points of view. But that has nothing to do with the support the Secretary of State gives to the Viceroy, and which you have given to me in a time of great difficulty, and for which I shall always be warmly grateful.

THE MARQUESS OF LANSDOWNE:—I think the noble Viscount will see from the report of my speech, that the part he has quoted had reference to measures of repression, and that what I said was that justice should be prompt, that it was undesirable that there should be appeals from one Court to another, or from Provincial Governments to the Government in Calcutta, or from the Government at Calcutta to the Secretary of State for India. I did not mean to imply merely the Viceroy, but the men responsible for local Government.

VISCOUNT MORLEY:—I do not think that when the noble Marquess refers to the report of his speech he will find I have misrepresented him. At all events, he will, I do believe, gladly agree that, in dealing with sedition, I have on the whole given all the support the Government of India or anybody else concerned had a right to ask for.

I will now say a word about the Indian Civil Service. Three years ago, when we began these operations, I felt that a vital condition of success was that we should carry the Indian Civil Service with us, and that if we did not do this, we should fail. But human nature being what it is, and temperaments varying as they do, it is natural to expect a certain amount of criticism, minute criticism, and observation. I have had that, but will content myself with one quotation from the Lieutenant-Governor of Bengal, well-known to the noble Lord opposite. What did he say, addressing the Legislative Council a few weeks ago?:—

> I hold that a solemn duty rests upon the officers of Government in all branches, and more particularly upon the officers of the Civil Service, so to comport themselves in the inception and working of the new measures as to make the task of the people and their leaders easy. It is incumbent upon them loyally to accept the principle that these measures involve the surrender of some portion of the authority and control which they now exercise, and some modifications of the methods of administration. If that task is approached in a grudging or reluctant spirit, we shall be sowing the seeds of failure, and shall forfeit our claim to receive the friendly co-operation of the representatives of the people. We must be prepared to support, defend, and carry through the administrative policy and in a certain degree even the executive acts of the Government in the Council, in much the same way as is now prescribed in regard to measures of legislation; and we must further be prepared to discharge this task without the aid of a standing majority behind us. We will have to resort to the more difficult arts of persuation and conciliation in the place of the easier methods of autocracy. This is no small demand to make on the resources of a service whose training and traditions have hitherto led its members rather to work for the people, than through the people or their representatives. But I am nevertheless confident that the demand will not be made in vain. For more than a hundred years, in the time of the Company and under the rule of the Crown, the Indian Civil Service has never failed to respond to whatever call has been made upon it or to adapt itself to the changing environment of the time. I feel no doubt that officers will be found who possess the natural gifts, the loyalty, the imagination, and the force of character which will be requisite for the conduct of the administration under the more advanced form of government to which we are about to succeed.

These words I commend to your Lordships. They breathe a fine and high spirit; they admirably express the feeling of a sincere man; and I do not believe anybody who is acquainted with the Service doubts that this spirit, so admirably expressed, will pervade the Service in the admittedly difficult task that now confronts them.

The Bill is a short one, and will speak for itself. I shall be brief in referring to it, for in December last I made what was practically a Second-Reading speech. I may point out that there are two rival schools, and that the noble Lord opposite (Lord Curzon) may be said to represent one of them. There are two rival schools, one of which believes that better government of India depends on efficiency, and that efficiency, is in fact, the main end of our rule in India. The other school, while not neglecting efficiency, looks also to what is called political concessions. I think I am doing the noble Lord no injustice in saying that, during his remarkable Viceroyalty, he did not accept the necessity for political concessions, but trusted to efficiency. I hope it will not be bad taste to say in the noble Lord's presence, that you will never send to India, and you have never sent to India, a Viceroy his superior, if indeed, his equal, in force of mind, in unsparing and remorseless industry, in passionate and devoted interest in all that concerns the well-being of India, with an imagination fired by the grandeur of the political problem that India presents—you never sent a man with more of all these attributes than when you sent Lord Curzon. But splendidly designed as was his work from the point of view of efficiency, he still left in India a state of things, when we look back upon it, that could not be held a satisfactory crowning of a brilliant and ambitious career.

I am as much for efficiency as the noble Lord, but I do not believe—and this is the difference between him and myself—that you can now have true, solid, endurable efficiency without what are called political concessions. I know the risks. The late Lord Salisbury, speaking on the last Indian Councils Bill, spoke of the risk of applying occidental machinery in India. Well, we ought to have thought of that before we applied occidental education; we applied that, and a measure of occidental machinery must follow. Legislative Councils once called into existence, then it was inevitable that you would have gradually, in Lord Salisbury's own phrase, to popularise them, so as to bring them into harmony with the dominant sentiments of the people in India. The Bill of 1892 admittedly contained the elective principle, and our Bill today extends that principle. The noble Lord (Viscount Cross) will remember the Bill of 1892, of which he had charge in the House of Commons. I want the House to be good enough to follow the line taken by Mr. Gladstone, because I base myself on that. There was an amendment moved and it was going to a division, but Mr. Gladstone begged his friends not to divide, because, he said, it was very important that we should present a substantial unity to India. This is upon the question of either House considering a Bill like the Bill that is now on the table—a mere skeleton of a Bill you like. I see it has been called vague and sketchy.

It cannot be anything else, on the broad principle set out by Mr. Gladstone:—

> It is the intention of the Government [that is, the Conservative Government] that a serious effort shall be made to consider carefully those elements which India in its present condition may furnish, for the introduction into the Councils of India of the elective principle. If that effort is seriously to be made, by whom is it to be made? I do not think it can be made, by this House, except through the medium of empowering provisions. The best course we could take would be to commend to the authorities of India what is a clear indication of the principles on which we desire them to proceed. It is not our business to devise machinery for the purpose of Indian Government. It is our business to give to those who represent Her Majesty in India ample information as to what we believe to be sound principles of Government: and it is, of course, the function of this House to comment upon any case, in which we may think they have failed to give due effect to those principles.

I only allude to Mr. Gladstone's words, in order to let the House know that I am taking no unusual course in leaving the bulk of the work, the details of the work, to the Government of India. Discussion, therefore, in Parliament will necessarily not, and cannot turn substantially upon details. But no doubt it is desirable that the main heads of the regulations, rules, and proclamations to be made by the Government of India under sanction of the India Office, should be more or less placed within the reach and knowledge of the House so far as they are complete. The principles of the Bill are in the Bill, and will be affirmed, if your Lordships are pleased to read it a second time. The Committee points, important as they are, can well be dealt with in Committee. The view of Mr. Gladstone was cheerfully accepted by the House of Commons then, and I hope it will be accepted by your Lordships to-day.

There is one very important chapter in these regulations, which I think now on the Second Reading of the Bill, without waiting for Committee, I ought to say a few words to your Lordships about—I mean the Mahomedans. That is a part of the Bill and scheme that has no doubt attracted a great deal of criticism, and excited a great deal of feeling in that important community. We suggested to the Government of India a certain plan. We did not prescribe it, we did not order it, but we suggested and recommended this plan for their consideration—no more than that. It was the plan of a mixed or composite electoral college, in which Mahomedans and Hindus should pool their votes, so to say. The wording of the recommendation in my despatch was, as I soon discovered, ambiguous—a grievous defect, of which I make bold to hope I am not very often in public business guilty. But, to the best of my belief, under any construction the plan of Hindus and Mahomedans voting together, in a mixed and composite electorate, would have secured to the Mahomedan electors, wherever they were so minded, the chance of returning their own representatives in their due proportion. The political idea at the bottom of this recommendation, which has found so little favour, was that such composite action would bring the two great communities more closely together, and this hope of promoting harmony was held by men of high Indian authority and experience who were among my advisers at the India Office. But the

Mahomedans protested that the Hindus would elect a pro-Hindu upon it, just as I suppose in a mixed college of say seventy-five Catholics and twenty-five Protestants voting together, the Protestants might suspect that the Catholics voting for the Protestant would choose what is called a Romanising Protestant, and as little of a Protestant as they could find. Suppose the other way. In Ireland there is an expression, a "shoneen" Catholic—that is to say, a Catholic who, though a Catholic, is too friendly with English Conservatism and other influences which the Nationalists dislike. And it might be said, if there were seventy-five Protestants against twenty-five Catholics, that the Protestants when giving a vote in the way of Catholic representation, would return "shoneens." I am not going to take your Lordships' time up by arguing this to-day. With regard to schemes of proportional representation, as Calvin said of another study: "Excessive study of the Apocalypse either finds a man mad, or makes him so." At any rate, the Government of India doubted whether our plan would work, and we have abandoned it. I do not think it was a bad plan, but it is no use, if you are making an earnest attempt in good faith at a general pacification, to let parental fondness for a clause interrupt that good process by sitting obstinately tight.

The Mahomedans demand three things. I had the pleasure of receiving a deputation from them, and I know very well what is in their minds. They demand the election of their own representatives to these

Councils in all the stages, just as in Cyprus, where I think, the Mahomedans vote by themselves. They have nine votes and the non-Mahomedans have three, or the other way about. So in Bohemia, where the Germans vote alone and have their own register. Therefore, we are not without a precedent and a parallel, for the idea of a separate register. Secondly, they want a number of seats somewhat in excess of their numerical strength. Those two demands we are quite ready and intend to meet in full. There is a third demand that, if there is a Hindu on the Viceroy's Executive Council—a subject on which I will venture to say something to your Lordships before I sit down—there should be two Indian members on the Viceroy's Council and one should be a Mahomedan. Well, as I told them and as I now tell your Lordships, I see no chance whatever of meeting their views in that way.

To go back to the point of the registers, some may be shocked at the idea of a religious register at all, a register framed on the principle of religious belief. We may wish—we do wish—that it were otherwise. We hope that time, with careful and impartial statesmanship, will make things otherwise. Only let us not forget that the difference between Mahomedanism and Hinduism is not a mere difference of articles of religious faith or dogma. It is a difference in life, in tradition, in history, in all the social things as well as articles of belief, that constitute a community. Do not let us forget what makes it interesting and even exciting. Do not let us forget that, in talking of Hindus and Mahomedans, we are dealing with, and are brought face to face with, vast historic issues. We are dealing with the very mightiest forces that through all the centuries and ages have moulded the fortunes of great States and the destinies of countless millions of mankind. Thoughts of that kind, my Lords, are what give to Indian politics and to Indian work extraordinary fascination, though at the same time they impose the weight of an extraordinary burden.

I come to the question which, I think, has excited certainly in this country, more interest than anything else in the scheme before you—I mean the question of an Indian member on the Viceroy's Executive Council. The noble Marquess said here the other day that he hoped an opportunity would be given for discussing it. Whether it is in order or not—I am too little versed in your Lordships' procedure to be quite sure—but I am told that the rules of order in this House are of an elastic description and that I shall not be trespassing beyond what is right, if I introduce the point to-night. I thoroughly understand Lord Lansdowne's anxiety for a chance of discussion. It is quite true, and the House should not forget it, that this question is in no way whatever touched by the Bill. If this Bill were rejected by Parliament, it would be a grievous disaster to peace and contentment in India, but it would not prevent the Secretary of State the very next morning from advising His Majesty to appoint an Indian member to the Viceroy's Executive Council.

The noble Marquess the other day fell into a slight error, if he will forgive me for saying so. He said that the Government of India had used caution and tentative words, indicating that it would be premature to decide at once this question of the Indian member until after further experience had been gained. I think the noble Marquess must have lost his way in the mazes of that enormous Blue-Book which, as he told us, caused him so much inconvenience, and added so much to his excess luggage during the Christmas holidays. The despatch, as far as I can discover, is silent altogether on the topic of the Indian member of the Viceroy's Council, and deals only with the Councils of Bombay and Madras and the proposed Councils for the Lieutenant-Governorships.

Perhaps, I might be allowed to remind your Lordships of the Act of 1833—certainly the most extensive and important measure of Indian Government between Mr. Pitt's famous Act of 1784, and Queen Victoria's assumption of the Government of India in 1858. There is nothing more important than that Act. It lays down in the broadest way possible the desire of Parliament that there should be no difference in appointing to offices in India between one race and another and the covering despatch written by that memorable man, James Mill, wound up by saying that :—

"For the future, fitness is to be the criterion of eligibility."

I need not quote the famous paragraph in the

Queen's Proclamation of 1858. Every Member of the House who takes an interest in India, knows that by heart. Now, the noble Marquess says that his anxiety is that nothing shall be done to impair the efficiency of the Viceroy's Council. I share that anxiety with all my heart. I hope the noble Marquess will do me the justice to remember that in these plans I have gone beyond the Government of India, in resolving that a permanent official majority shall remain in the Viceroy's Council. Lord MacDonnell said the other day:—

> I believe you cannot find any individual native gentleman who is enjoying general confidence, who would be able to give advice and assistance to the Governor-General in Council.

Well, for that matter, it has been my lot twice to fill the not very exhilarating post of Chief Secretary for Ireland, and I do not believe I can truly say I ever met in Ireland a single individual native gentleman who "enjoyed general confidence." And yet I received at Dublin Castle most excellent and competent advice. Therefore, I am not much impressed by that argument. The question is whether there is no one of the 300 millions of the population of India, who is competent to be the officially-constituted adviser of the Governor-General in Council in the administration of Indian affairs. You make an Indian a Judge of the High Court, and Indians have even been acting Chief Justices. As to capacity, who can deny that they have distinguished themselves as administrators of Native States, where a very full demand is made on their resources, intellectual and moral? It is said that the presence of an Indian member would cause restraint in the language of discussion. For a year-and-a-half we have had two Indians on the Council of India, and we have none of us ever found the slightest restraint.

Then there is the question : What are you going to do about the Hindu and the Mahomedan ? When Indians were first admitted to the High Courts, for a long time the Hindus were more fit and competent than the Mahomedans ; but now I am told the Mahomedans have their full share. The same sort of operation would go on in quinquennial periods in respect of the Viceroy's Council. Opinion amongst the great Anglo-Indian officers now at home is divided, but I know at least one, not at all behind Lord MacDonnell in experience or mental grasp, who is strongly in favour of this proposal. One circumstance that cannot but strike your Lordships as remarkable, is the comparative absence of hostile criticism of this idea by the Anglo-Indian Press, and, as I am told, in Calcutta society. I was apprehensive at one time that it might be otherwise. I should like to give a concrete illustration of my case. The noble Marquess opposite said the other day that there was going to be a vacancy in one of the posts on the Viceroy's Executive Council—that is, the Legal Member's time would soon be up. Now, suppose there were in Calcutta an Indian lawyer of large practice and great experience in his profession—a man of unstained professional and personal repute, in close touch with European society, and much respected, and the actual holder of important legal office. Am I to say to this man:

> In spite of all these excellent circumstances to your credit; in spite of your undisputed fitness; in spite of the emphatic declaration of 1833 that fitness is to be the criterion of eligibility; in spite of the noble promise in Queen Victoria's Proclamation of 1858—a promise of which every Englishman ought to be for ever proud if he tries to adhere to it, and ashmed if he tries to betray or to mock it—in spite of all this, usage and prejudice are so strong, that I dare not appoint you, but must instead fish up a stranger to India from Lincoln's Inn or the Temple?

Is there one of your Lordships who would envy the Secretary of State, who had to hold language of that kind to a meritorious candidate, one of the King's equal subjects? I press it on your Lordships in that concrete way. Abstract general arguments are slippery. I do not say there is no force in them, but there are deeper questions at issue to which both I and the Governor-General attach the greatest importance. My Lords, I thank you for your attention, and I beg to move the Second Reading.

THE CREATION OF PROVINCIAL EXECUTIVE COUNCILS.

[*In the House of Lords on Tuesday, March 9th 1909, on the order for the report stage of this Bill being read, Viscount Morley moved an amendment regarding the creation of Executive Councils.*]

Viscount Morley of Blackburn said:—I have now to move an amendment. It is in effect, the full restitution of what was third clause (Power to create Provincial Executive Councils), which your Lordships rejected on Thursday last. I hope your Lordships will believe that in moving what is in effect the restoration of this third clause I am not animated by any particular pertinacity. Of course, I regretted the rejection of the clause, and I regret it still, and I have a particular reason for regretting it, because I understand from authorities in India that the effect there is unfortunate—that is the word—that the effect of the rejection of this clause is unfortunate, very unfortunate. I am sure every noble Lord in the House is keenly alive to the cardinal importance of the way in which the people of India—all the various communities which make up what we call India—watch what we are doing at home here in the India Office and in Parliament, and it is above all things desirable that we should allow no impression to get abroad in India that we are negligent in looking at the real effect of what we are doing. Feeling this, and observing that both the noble Marquis, the leader of the Opposition, and the noble Lord opposite, Lord Curzon were careful to say—and Lord Curzon has repeated it in a letter which appeared in the *Times* on Saturday—that they have no rooted objection to the principle of the clause, that their resistance to the clause was not meant to be of a permanent kind, and the noble Marquis even suggested that we should by-and-bye, in the course of the present Session I think he said, bring up that clause in the form of a Parliamentary Bill. I telegraphed to the Government of India and to the Viceroy as to their views. I thought it was just to Parliament and to your Lordships to find out what their view was, because as I understood, the objection of noble Lords opposite, of Lord Lansdowne and Lord Curzon, and of my noble friend on the cross bench, was founded upon this, that the opinion of the Government and authorities in India had not been effectively ascertained.

THE GOVERNMENT OF INDIA AND EXECUTIVE COUNCILS.

I have now received a reply to that inquiry of mine. With your Lordships' permission I am not going to argue as to the merits of the clause. That was argued adequately and sufficiently in Committee. I am not going to say a word about the arguments for or against the clause. I have to communicate to your Lordships the views of the Government of India. These are not the exact words of the telegram, for reasons which the noble Marquis will understand, but it is as good as a textual reproduction:

> The Government in 1905—that' was before the present Government took office—" discussed the question of Provincial Executive Councils. At that time their opinion was adverse to the introduction of Councils in Provinces administered by Lieutenant-Governors; but since then conditions have changed and they are still changing. Our opinion now is that the arguments then used against Government by Executive Councils are not any longer of the same force. When the constitutional changes now proposed in the Bill which your Lordships read the second time a few days ago—come into operation the situation will be different, and that is our reason for modifying our views. There must then, under the new conditions, be a large increase in the work of Lieutenant-Governors, and we anticipate it will be necessary to give them some kind of further assistance, not only in respect of the actual work of these Legislative Councils, but also with a view to relieving the Lieutenant-Governors, of minor executive matters. We refer to this point in paragraph 76 of our despatch of October 1, as it came under consideration when the general question of reform was being examined. There are already very great calls made upon the time of Lieutenant-Governors—and so forth—and there can be no doubt that indirectly the enlargement of Legislative Councils proposed in this Bill will multiply the occasions requiring the Lieutenant-Governors to deal with questions of public importance. We consider that, in all probability, the best means of giving the required assistance will prove to be the creation of Executive Councils. The members of such a Council would be responsible Ministers who could speak in the matter of Government in a way that no secretaries or other officials could do. For the reason we have given we are in favour of having the power proposed by clause 3 in the Bill, and we should regret if the opportunity which now presents itself of obtaining that power for us were to be lost. We are altogether opposed to the proposal which we understand has been put forward to create forthwith Councils in all the larger Provinces, and we desire to make that point clear. We see no present necessity for a general change of this character, and it should be made, if it is to be made, only in the light of experience. That clause 3 would give us. We should exercise the power given under clause 3 gradually and cautiously and only after the fullest consideration of the effect of the new conditions in such Province.

Now, my Lords, that is the position taken up by the Government of India. That is the request, if I may so call it, that they address to Parliament—namely, that we should take this opportunity of giving them those powers, of caution in exercising which they give an assurance that I know every noble Lord in the House will thoroughly trust. I submit that it would be prudent for this House not to postpone this. The noble Marquis opposite says: Postpone it. Why? We all know that what happens in a Session of Parliament. Supposing towards July the noble Marquis will say: Now the time has come when we could give the Indian Government the powers which we refused them in March. I cannot think that is a business-like, or politic course. I cannot think on what substantial grounds he will resist my proposal to re-insert the clause giving the Government of India powers which the noble Marquis does not deny might, with a little more experience, be useful, and which, as I say, will be used cautiously and carefully.

CLOSING SPEECH ON THE SECOND READING OF THE INDIAN COUNCILS BILL.

[*On the order for going into Committee on the Indian Councils Bill, on Tuesday March 4th*, 1909.]

Viscount Morley of Blackburn said he desired to make one or two observations. The debate on the second reading was a very remarkable one in many respects. There was, if he might say so, great knowledge shown. Noble Lords with enormous experience and knowledge of India gave the House the benefit of their opinions on the Bill, and he was bound to say that the criticism was perfectly fair and that it was made in a temper towards the Bill and towards those who were responsible for it of which no kind of complaint could be made. He thought Lord Middleton had described truly the mood of the House when, in an early sentence of his most interesting speech, he said the House and the country had come to a position when we had to face the fact, and that the facts we had to face make it impossible either to stand still or not to make a move in advance. He believed that the passing of the second reading of the Bill without a division was a sign of the sense that that House had of the peculiarity and gravity of the situation we had to meet. It was inevitable, in such a situation, and with a Bill of the magnitude and importance of this, that the authors of the Bill should have to face a great deal of criticism and observations, and two or three noble Lords opposite, and one or two behind him, did criticise the Bill and make points of objection to this or that feature in it. It was impossible to bring forward any Bill whatever, whether a very moderate Bill or a fuller Bill such as the one they were now talking about, without exposing a good deal of surface criticism; but, having carefully studied and weighed all the points that were made on the second reading, he did not feel that the foundation or substance of the Bill had been damaged, or that any good reason had been shown why they should not proceed with it, and proceed with it with a determination—this was a very important point—not to whittle it away in Committee, not to defeat the effect which, as Lord Curzon had admitted, it had had of relaxing the tension in India. He hoped, therefore, that nothing done in Committee would impair that most desirable consequence.

THE CHARGE OF RUSHING THE BILL.

It was said that he, as the responsible Minister, had rushed the Bill, or, at all events, some points of it, and he had seen it stated in some of the Indian telegrams that there was a frantic haste in the consideration of this measure. He could not imagine what people could mean who considered the facts. It was three years ago since this policy was, as it were, put on the anvil. The Government of India sent a despatch containing their views of the policy which they hoped might be embodied in a measure so far as Parliamentary sanction was necessary. The Government at home sent them back a reply begging them to reconsider this or that point and to submit the whole case to the local Governments and local authorities. That was done. It took a very long time, but it was very carefully and even exhaustively done. The end of it was a second despatch in October of last year. The Government at home considered it again, and they made certain modifications in it. But those were not hastily made. Did any one believe that an Indian Secretary—was there any one of the 15 men who had held the office of Indian Secretary—who would have dreamed of framing and completing a measure of this importance without consultation with the Viceroy and the Government of India? It was quite impossible and not conceivable, and he could only say that he was entirely guiltless of the frantic haste and hurry of which he was sometimes definitely accused. Lord Lansdowne had pointed to the last stage of all, and referred to his requirement, so to call it, from the Government of India, that their views, so far as the heads of the regulations were concerned, should be in his possession when he had to move the second reading of the Bill in their Lordships' House. It was quite true that no great length of time was given for the consideration of those proposals to be framed afterwards in the regulations. But the local authorities had had all the topics before them for three years. They had had, he thought, two solemn and formal inquisitions into them, and had given a great deal of evidence to the Decentralisation Commission, much of that evidence touching points now in the Bill. The air had been full of all the topics for three years, and surely, then, there was nothing unreasonable or hurrying in asking these gentlemen and the authorities they represented what they thought as to the line of this or that regulation. He hoped, therefore, that noble Lord opposite, and their Lordships at large, would absolve him from having been hasty at all. On the contrary, no one could have been more deliberate or more anxious to have consultation with the Government of India than he was, and he did not believe that anybody there would say otherwise.

WHAT REGULATIONS HAVE BEEN DECIDED UPON.

He had promised, in reply to the request made to him, that he would on this occasion describe to the House, so far as he could, the general heads of the regulations so far as they had yet arrived in discussing and settling them. Everybody agreed that it was for the Government of India to shape and frame these regulations in conformity with principles laid down at home, but not arrived at without full consultation and deliberation with them. He would state first the points already settled which were to be dealt with by regulations, rules, or proclamations. The first regulation already settled fixed the number of members of the Imperial Council and the Councils of Madras, Bombay, Bengal, the United Provinces, Eastern

Bengal, Punjab and Burma. He would not trouble their Lordships with the number, but they were fixed.

THE MARQUIS OF LANSDOWNE: Do they approximate to the maximum laid down in the schedule?

Viscount Morely said he was not sure that they did. The number of the Imperial Council was to be 65, including the Viceroy; Madras, Bombay, Bengal, and United Provinces, 47 each; Eastern Bengal, 37; Punjab, 25; and Burma, 17. The next point was the quorum whieh was fixed at 21 for the Imperial Council; 15 for Madras, Bombay, Bengal, and United Provinces; 12 for Eastern Bengal; and eight for Punjab and Burma. The third point settled was the term of office, which was three years for ordinary members and one year or less for the class known as experts. They had settled too, the method of filling casual vacancies. In the case of casual vacancies to be filled by election, the proper body or group of bodies would be informed of the vacancy by the head of the Government and requested to elect a member. If no such member was elected within three months of the date of receiving the request, the head of the Government might then nominate, at his discretion, a person belonging to the community or local area which the body or group of bodies was supposed to represent.

THE BUDGET DEBATE SETTLED IN PRINCIPLE.

He came to the second head—rules settled, in principle. The discussion of the annual financial statement was the most important branch of the new system. He need not dwell upon this system, because it was described very fully and clearly in the Blue-Book, and it was not easy to summarise. Coming to the Imperial financial statement, the Legislative Council would resolve itself into Committee and discuss it by heads sitting *de die in diem* till it was finished. Each item would be explained by the member in charge, and every member might move resolutions and divide the Committee on them; such resolutions being in the form of recommendations to the Government, who, of course, were not bound any more than they were either in their Lordships' House or in another place to take action upon them. When the Committee had finished, the Government would make such alterations in the Budget as it thought fit, and the Budget in its final form would be submitted to the Council, when there would be a general discussion and no more resolutions. All through, certain items of revenue and expenditure, including the State Railways and the Army, were excluded from the debate. That was a very important limitation. The discussion on the Provincial Budgets would be on somewhat similar lines, except that a standing Committee of the Council would be appointed not more than 12 in number, and equally divided between officials and non-officials, to consider the Estimates in a private and informal manner, in their first stage. In their second stage, the Council would resolve itself into Committee; and in the third stage the Council as such would discuss them, as in the case of the Imperial Council. The subjects of general interest would be discussed subject to the following conditions, which had not yet been put into the form of rules; (1) Resolutions must relate to matters of public and general importance; (2) no resolution should of itself have any force or effect; (3) the order of business was to be under the entire control of the President; (4) the President to have power to disallow any resolution if, in his opinion, it was contrary to public policy; (5) certain classes of subjects, to be defined when the rules of the business were drafted, to be expressly excluded. So much for the matters that were settled in principle.

MATTERS REMAINING FOR DETERMINATION.

The Bill left the following points to be dealt with by regulations, rules or proclamation. There were three possible ways of proceeding—regulation, rules (a narrower instrument), and proclamation, which only arose in two or three cases. The points to be dealt with were:—(1) The number of members, only the maximum being fixed by the Bill; (2) the number of a quorum; (3) the term of office; (4) the manner of filling casual vacancies; (5) the conditions under which and the manner in which, persons resident in India might be nominated or elected; (6) the qualifications for being nominated or elected a member. There were rules not yet settled affecting the discussion of the annual financial statement, and the asking of questions. As to the Executive Councils, they were called into existence by proclamation, and they were now considering—and the Government of India especially—what powers of the Lieutenant-Governor should be exercised by the Lieutenant-Governor in Council, the number of the members of Council, their powers and duties, and the way of appointing temporary and acting members.

THE MANNER OF ELECTION.

The next question was the regulations still under consideration. All that had been decided as to the manner of election—and this, of course, affected the burning question of Mahomedan representation—was that there was to be election in the proper and natural sense. The ordinary way for nomination was for the Viceroy or Lieutenant-Governor to ratify the recommendation. The question arose: Ought they to persevere with that system, and still retain what was called nomination, but what was really ratification or confirmation in the case of members elected? The view of the Government was that it would make election rather—he did not say farcical in effect, but it would certainly make it look farcical if, after expanding the Act of 1892 in order to carry further the principle of election they reserved to executive authorities the power of saying whether election should be void or should be a valid choice. The Government had decided that there was to be no ratification.

DISQUALIFICATIONS.

Of course, that led to the necessity of going into the question of qualification. Every legislative body —certainly the House of Commons—exercised its right of excluding from membership within it persons coming within certain categories. The Government had not yet quite settled what those disqualifications were to be, and the Government of India in a telegram about ten days ago had provisionally proposed the following as disqualified persons:—(1) Females (*laughter*); (2) persons of unsound mind; (3) persons under 25 years of age; (4) insolvents, subject to the conditions which existed in our own country in the matter of bankruptcy; (5) persons who had been convicted of a non-bailable offence, when such sentence had not subsequently been quashed or reversed; (6) persons who had been dismissed from the service of the Government and declared ineligible for employment under the Government in future.

THE "RAGGED EDGE" OF DEPORTATION.

The Government of India were now specially considering a question undoubtedly of great moment—namely whether the persons dealt with under Regulation 3 under the Act of 1818, should be declared for ever disqualified. Nine or more persons were now deported under that regulation. He slipped into an error the other day in replying to Lord Middleton on this subject. He did not now bind himself to take the view he then expressed. He thought it required a great deal of consideration. All these questions of disqualifications had come into prominence because of the cessation of the ratification and confirmation from executive authorities. The moment they arrested that process it became necessary to lay down rules and categories of exclusion. In regard to all these categories and in the question of the deported men and so forth, he hoped the House would take the counsel which Lord Courtney gave the other day, and which, he confessed, he had much at heart. He thought it was vital for the success of this policy and this measure. If they were going to give these great extensions of power, let them not do it in a grudging way. If they made their list of disqualifications too large, if they included certain classes of people in India, he was afraid it would leave what he might call a " ragged edge " behind. It was vital that they should leave as little ragged edge as possible, if ragged edge there were at all. Of course, it was necessary to make provision to meet the case of corruption in elections. On any member becoming disqualified under any of these heads, the head of the Government would have power to declare his seat vacant. It was proposed by the Government of India that the oath or declaration of allegiance should be taken by every nominated or elective member before he took his seat, and unless he did so he should not be qualified to sit.

SUPPLEMENTARY QUESTIONS.

As to the rules as to questions, there were already rules on this subject, and the only important alteration would probably be in respect of supplementary questions. They heard a great deal in the debate on the second reading as to the evils that would arise from a promiscuous multitude of supplementary questions, such as they were familiar with in this country. Upon this rule no final decision had been arrived at, but it was proposed as follows:—

> No discussion shall be permitted in respect to an answer under this rule. A member may be permitted to ask a question for the elucidation of a matter of fact or of information asked for. The President may disallow a supplementary question without giving a reason for doing so.

That was the last explanation with which he need trouble the House as to the purport and scope of the rules and regulations, and he hoped the noble Marquis would consider he had explained them pretty fully. (*Cheers.*)

THIRD READING OF THE INDIAN COUNCILS BILL.

[*In the House of Lords, on Thursday, March* 11, 1909, *Viscount Morley of Blackburn, in moving the third reading of this Bill, said* :—]

This motion brings us, not I dare say to the last, but certainly to a decisive stage in this legislation. The importance of this legislation has been much dwelt upon by noble lords opposite, and I hope they will believe that no one recognises more fully than I do the responsibility that we all take in passing this Bill. I accept, not the anticipations of noble lords opposite, but I accept their views that the operations which may follow the passing of this law will be, in one direction or another, of a serious character well deserving of our fullest attention. I must say that, with one exception, I have no complaint to offer of the tone and scope of the criticisms which noble lords opposite who are so competent to speak on Indian affairs bestowed upon our proposals. They were, I think, open to a perfect answer; but the true answer, after all, will be found in the events that follow the working of the Act. We, for our part—and when I say we, I hope I may be allowed to include not only His Majesty's Government here but the Government of India—anticipate from this Act the most beneficent results. If things should take an untoward turn, the responsibility would not lie alone with us. I think the fact that noble lords opposite did not divide against the second reading—with which I have not the slightest intention of taunting them—shows, I think, they feel that the responsibility of rejecting our proposals would be a very grave and serious responsibility from which in the legitimate discharge of their public and patriotic duty they naturally shrink.

CLAUSE THREE.

I said there was one exception to my absence of complaint. I am not going to travel again at length over the ground of my complaint as to the rejection of the third clause of the Bill. The other day I said that authorities in India had telegraphed to me that they regarded that rejection as an unfortunate incident. I see in some prints that I ought to have mentioned who those authorities were; and there was an implication that they were authorities of no particular account. The authority—I do not know why I should not mention it—was the Viceroy. The Viceroy's judgment the day after the rejection of the clause took place was that the rejection of the clause was unfortunate, and I have since seen language used by a very important person that it was disastrous. I have been blamed for bringing again before your Lordships the third clause two or three days after it had been thrown out. I am assured that it was an unusual course in your Lordships' House; but I thought it my duty in fairness to the House that, after they had thrown out the clause, they should know and be guided by the knowledge and, as I hope, the impression of the result of that proceeding in India. It was through no pertinacity or stubbornness, however, to force my own proposal upon the House, because I have felt all through the proceedings since the debate began that this is not the case of an ordinary party Bill, and noble lords opposite have not treated it in that spirit. I cordially admit that, of course, as Lord Curzon reminded your Lordships and His Majesty's Government that the resources of civilization are not entirely exhausted by the rejection of the clause in your Lordships' House, and it may be as Lord Curzon hinted, that another opportunity at a not considerably later date may be given to this House to examine the arguments for that clause and the position in which that proposal stands.

CONSULTATIONS WITH INDIAN SPOKESMEN.

I turn for a moment with great reluctance to a sort of semi-personal point. Language is used in public prints, and I hear something of it even in private conversation, that there has been some mystification on my part, and random and schoolboy innuendoes are thrown out, almost lurid descriptions are sometimes drawn, as to the origin and source of this Bill. I must apologize for taking up your Lordships' time with a matter of this kind, but still it is best in an important proceeding of this sort, that all who take an interest in this subject—and there must be, I hope, many thousands of people who do take an interest—should know how this matter has proceeded. What do people mean when they say that reforms were wrung from the Secretary of State by an Indian political leader—a certain Indian political leader well-known to some of your Lordships? I ask the House, was it not the business of a Secretary of State or a Viceroy when undertaking a great scheme for improving a local Government in India, was it not the business of those two responsible Ministers to gather opinion upon proper details of such a scheme from every source, official and unofficial? (*Cheers.*) If you are going to try to improve the administration of a country, is a Minister, whether at Whitehall or at Simla, to shut his eyes and ears to opinion from every source and to the very persons who may be most concerned by the right or wrong, the expediency or inexpediency, the sense or folly of his measures? Is there a single member of your Lordships' House, however he may doubt the policy of this Bill, who will deny for a moment that the business of a Minister or a Viceroy was to hear opinion on every side?

Now, Mr. Gokhale, who is well known as a prominent and responsible spokesman of a very highly important section or branch of Indian opinion, came to see me at the India Office before the despatch of the Government of India of October last reached this country. I wound up our conversation with a request, which I have made to other people, that he would be so good as to write on a sheet of notepaper his views as to the reforms which he and his friends desire, and he did so on the spot. The very self-same process I went through with a spokesman of the Mahomedans. He visited me, I made to him the same request, and he complied in the same way. I do not call that wringing a measure from a Minister; and, if it is worth mentioning, I may say that I never had any communication whatever after that—which I think, was on some day in September—with Mr. Gokhale until the day before he left this country—after my despatch had gone—when he called to say good-bye. What did I do with those two notes? I followed in every proceeding connected with this policy, and especially with this Bill, the ordinary regular official course with one exception, which I will mention in a moment. No proceeding was ever more strictly in order, was ever more above broad, no transaction ever went through the not very exhilarating precincts of Whitehall more strictly in accord with ordinary rule and procedure. What happened? Those two notes and a great quantity of other material were laid before a Committee. Here was the exception that I made to the ordinary procedure. Before the Indian despatch arrived I received a summary of its contents from the Government of India, and I appointed a Committee from the Council of India, and I was able to invite to that Committee *amicus curise* the noble lord who sits behind me. [Lord MacDonnel indicated dissent.] They had these communications before them. I was not present. Then came the despatch of the Government of India, and that was discussed in the most strict conformity with the ordinary procedure of the India Office. It was referred to the appropriate Committee. Two or three members from the Council were added to the Committee, and they threshed out the despatch, and came to the conclusions which ultimately formed the basis of my despatch of November last. That is the whole story. I only regret that I did not see a great many more Indians. I saw all that I could; I wish I could have seen more. So much for that.

RELATIONS BETWEEN THE TWO GOVERNMENTS.

Then we are charged with not paying attention enough to the Government of India. I will not go into the constitutional and statutory relations between the Secretary of State and the Government of India. They are well known. They are beyond cavil and dispute. This is no occasion for opening that subject, and I hope for my own part that no such occasion will ever arise, because there are *arcana Imperii* which it is not expedient, I think, to make matter of debate in Parliament. The case of the relative rights and duties of the Secretary of State and the Viceroy does not arise because I doubt if ever there was in the history of discussion between two Ministers, heads of powerful departments, a discussion such as the Government of India and we have carried on for a great many months, but closely and constantly during the last two months, carried on with a more complete absence of the spirit of contention. (*Hear, hear.*) I say that—and my words will be open to public scrutiny or the scrutiny of those who know all the secrets, such secrets as there are—without any misgiving or hesitation of the spirit in which we have worked together. The only thing I am going at this moment to read is in my despatch of November to the Government of India, replying to their despatch, in which I applauded, recognized, and thanked them for their industry, patience, thought, and candour. And then I say: "It is a sincere satisfaction to me to find myself able to accept the substantial part of your Excellency's scheme, with such modifications as would naturally occur to different minds"—the Governor-General in Council and the Secretary of State in Council—" handling problems of remarkable difficulty in themselves and reasonably open to a wide variety of interpretation." That spirit, which animated both myself in Council and the Governor-General-in-Council, has gone on unabated and unimpaired, and if there are points that we have pressed that they would not of themselves have proposed there has been no serious demur. If there had been serious demur to such a proposal as, for example, that of the official majorities or the proposal to take power to appoint Executive Councils in the great Provinces, I should have been shaken. Therefore, I hope the House will believe that these, I will not say arguments, but these innuendoes—I am not accusing the noble Marquis of stooping to that—of which I hear so much are really random, undeserved, and complete moonshine.

INDIAN POLITICAL LEADERS AND OUTRAGES.

I have no more to say about the Bill except this. It has been admitted all through—the noble Marquis has not denied it, and Lord Curzon expressly admitted it—that we had reason to congratulate ourselves so far on the fact that the introduction of the Bill and the announcement of the policy which it was my fortune to make in your Lordships' House in December have produced a remarkable abatement in the tension, which was formerly a source of difficulty and embarassment to Lord Minto's Government. Without making a boast—it is too early yet—as to the effect of the Bill I think the House will be interested to know of the account I received on March 6. I cannot reproduce the text but I hope your Lordships will allow me to convey to you the substance of it. It bears on the Bill and on the public mind in this country in judging the Bill.

The insinuation that Indian political leaders are still unwilling to denounce outrages is not the case. So I am assured. Immediately after murder of the Counsel [the hateful murder the other day of the prosecuting Counsel in the Court] an influential native meeting was held in the Town Hall of Calcutta to protest against the outrage. The Moderates are quite genuine in their wish to assist in putting down anarchy. India is not, so I am assured and readily believe, and all the evidence points in the same way, in a state of insurrection. That is not to say that we may not expect further isolated attempts at outrage. The Government of India do not believe them to be instigated by any political party of the least importance. Any further outrages which may probably occur at intervals would in no way indicate widespread sedition or justify a belief in the disloyalty of the political leaders. The position now is really one for police watchfulness. Isolated outrages will not in any way justify {I commend this to any of your Lordships who doubt the policy of the Bill or have misgivings in connection with it] the assumption that the general state of the country is dangerous.

I hope the House will think that that is a very satisfactory state of things. Language of that sort could not have been used six months ago. I am not taking credit for that improved state of things entirely to the Bill, but I am very earnest in pressing on your Lordships, as I have done all through the stages of the Bill, this fact—that any interruption or whittling away or retardation of this Bill will do something to impair what is satisfactory in the account I have just had the honour of communicating to your Lordships. I beg to move that this Bill be read a third time. (*Cheers.*)

THE HINDU MAHOMEDAN PROBLEM.

[*Lord Morley received at the India Office on Wednesday (January 27, 1909), a deputation of the London Branch of the All-India Moslem League, who waited upon him in order to represent to him the views of the Mussalmans of India on the projected Indian Reforms.*]

Lord Morley in reply said:—It is not too strong an expression to say that I am delighted to meet you to-day, because I have always felt in my political experience, which is now pretty long, that it is when face answers to face that you come in that way to points of controversial issue. I have listened to the very able speech of my friend, Mr. Ameer Ali and to the speech which followed with close attention, not merely for the sake of the arguments upon the special points raised, but—what is more important than the special points very often and, I am sure, in this case—because the underlying feeling and the animating spirit of those two speeches are to me full of encouragement. Why? Because instead of—as I rather anticipated, or did till a few days ago—a rather hostile attitude to our reforms as a whole, I find that you receive them and welcome them cordially and with gratitude. I cannot say with what satisfaction I received that announcement, and how much it encourages me. If you will allow me, I will, before I come to the special points, say a few words upon the general position, because it is very important to you and to us of His Majesty's Government.

A HOPEFUL OUTLOOK.

It is only five weeks, I think, since our scheme was launched, and I am bound to say that at the end of those five weeks the position may fairly be described as most hopeful and most promising. (*Hear, hear.*) I do not think that the millennium will come in five more weeks, nor in 50 weeks; but I do say that for a scheme of so wide a scope to be received as this scheme has been is a very promising and hopeful sign. It does not follow that because we have launched our ship with a slant of fair wind that means the same thing as getting into harbour. There are plenty of difficult points which we have got to settle, but when I try from my conning tower in this office to look round and read the signs in the political skies, I, for one, am full of hope and confidence. The great thing is that in every party both in India and at home—in every party, and every section, and every group—there is a recognition of the magnitude and the gravity of the enterprise on which we have embarked; and that will have a very remarkable effect. I studied very closely the proceedings at Madras; and I studied the proceedings at Amritsar, and in two most able speeches made in both those places I find a truly political spirit in the right sense of the word—in the sense of perspective and proportion—which I sometimes wish could be imitated by some of my excellent English friends. I mean that issues important enough but upon which some differences are put aside—for the time only, if you like, but still put aside—in face of and considering the magnitude of the great issues which we present to you in these reforms. On Monday, in the *Times* newspaper, there was a very long and most interesting communication from Bombay, written I believe, by a gentleman of very wide Indian knowledge and even, level-headed humour. Now, what does he say? He takes account of the general position as he found it in India shortly after the despatch arrived.

"I might have dwelt," he says, "upon the fact that I have not met a single official who does not admit that some changes which should gratify Indian longings were necessary, and I might have expatiated upon the abounding evidence that Lord Morley's despatch and speech have unquestionably eased a tension which had become exceedingly alarming."

That is a very important thing, which I believe Parliament has recognised—certainly it is recognised in the Cabinet.

THE NECESSITY FOR OFFICIAL SUPPORT.

We are not free to do altogether what we would like. We cannot fold our arms and say that things are to go on as they did before, and I rejoice to see what this gentleman says there. He is talking of officials, and—I speak quite frankly—I always felt from the beginning that if we did not succeed in carrying with us the goodwill of that most important and powerful service, the Indian Civil Service, there would be good reason for suspecting that we were wrong upon the merits, and even if we were not wrong on the merits, there would be good reason for apprehending formidable difficulties. I have myself no end of confidence in them. I sometimes see in some journals of my own party suspicions thrown upon the loyalty of that service to His Majesty's Government of the day, whoever and whatever that Government may be. It is absurd to think anything of the kind. If our policy and our proposals receive the approval of Parliament and the approval of officials, such as those spoken of in the *Times* the other day, I am perfectly sure there will be no more want of goodwill and zeal on the part of the Indian Civil Service than there would be in the officers of His Majesty's Fleet or His Majesty's Army—it would be just the same. I should like to read another passage from that letter :—

> It would probably be incorrect to say that the bulk of the Civil Service in the Bombay Presidency are gravely apprehensive. Most of them are not unnaturally anxious—I agree; it is perfectly natural that they should be anxious—but the main officials in whose judgment most confidence can be placed regard the future with the buoyant hopefulness without which an Englishman in India is lost indeed.

I think all that is reassuring, and no sign nor whisper reaches me that any responsible section or creed, either in India or here, has any desire whatever—except wrong-headed individuals; such individuals exist, I daresay, even in India—to wreck our scheme. That is a very important position to start from. And let us go further. We could not have a better sign—I am always told to realise the magnitude of what we are about, that statesmen abroad outside these realms capable of reflection are watching us with interest and wishing us well—than the remarkable and splendid utterance of President Roosevelt the other day at Washington. And if we turn from Washington to the East, in Europe, I know very well that any injustice, any suspicion that we were capable of being unjust to Mahomedans in India would certainly have a very severe and injurious reaction in Constantinople. (*Hear, hear.*) I am alive to all these things. Mr. Ameer Ali said he was sure the Secretary of State would mete out just and equitable treatment to all interests if their views were fairly laid before him. That gentleman did me no more than justice when he said that. The Government are most zealous and earnest, acting in thorough good faith, in the desire to press forward these proposals. I may tell you that our Bill, which will be submitted to Parliament, its assent being necessary, is ready. I will introduce it at the first minute after the address is over, and, when it reaches other places, it will be pressed forward with all the force and resolution that Parliamentary conditions permit. There will be no time lost. These are not mere pious opinions or academic reforms; they are proposals which are to take Parliamentary shape, at the earliest possible moment; and after taking Parliamentary shape, no time will, I know, be lost in India in bringing them as rapidly as possible into practical operation.

THE MAHOMEDANS' COMPLAINT.

Now the first point Mr. Ameer Ali made was upon

the unfairness to the members of the Mahomedan community, caused by reckoning in the Hindu census a large multitude of men who are—not entitled to be there, in short. I cannot for many reasons follow that argument. I submit that it is not very easy—and I have gone into the question very carefully—to divide these lower castes and to classify them. Statisticians would be liable to be charged with putting too many into either one or the other division, wherever you like to draw the line. I know the force of the argument, and am willing to attach to it whatever weight it deserves. I wish some of my friends in this country would study the figures of what are called the lower castes, because they would then see the enormous difficulty and absurdity—absurdity—of applying to India the same principles that are very good guides to us Westerners who have been bred on the pure milk of the Benthamite word—one man one vote and every man a vote. That dream, by the way, is not quite realised yet in this country; but the idea of insisting on a principle of that sort—and I should not be surprised if my friend here (Mr. Buchanan) heard something of it before he is many weeks older—is absurd to anybody who reflects on the multiplicity of these varied castes.

THE PROPOSED ELECTORAL COLLEGES.

Then there is the question of the joint electorate —what is called the mixed electoral college. I was very glad to read this paragraph in the paper that you were good enough to send to me. You recognise the very principle which was at the back of our minds when we came to the conclusion of the mixed electoral college. You say:

> In common with other well-wishers of India the Committee look forward to a time when the development of a true spirit of compromise or the fusion of the races may make principles indicated by his Lordship capable of practical application without sacrificing the interests of any of the nationalities or giving political ascendancy to one to the disadvantage of the others. But the Committee venture to think that, however ready the country may be for constitutional reforms the interest of the two great communities of India must be considered and dealt with separately.

Therefore, to begin with, the difference between us in principle about the joint electorate is only this. We are guilty of nothing more than that we were premature, in the views of these gentlemen we were impatient idealists. You say to me: "It is very fine; we hope it will all come true, but you are premature; we must wait." But though premature I observe that your own suggestion in one of those papers adopts and accepts the principle of the scheme outlined in our despatch. It is quite true to say: "Oh, but you are vague in your despatch;" but a despatch is not a Bill. A Minister writing a despatch does not put in all the clauses and sections and sub-sections and schedules. It is the business of a Minister composing a despatch like ours of November 27, 1908, to indicate only general lines—general enough to make the substance and body of the scheme intelligible, but still general. I should like to say a word about the despatch. It is constantly assumed that in the despatch we prescribed and ordered the introduction of the joint electoral college. If any of you will be good enough to look at the despatch, you will find that no language of that sort—no law of the Medes and Persians—is to be found in it. If you refer to paragraph 12 you will see that our language is this:

> I suggest for your consideration that the object in view might be better secured, at any rate in the more advanced provinces in India, by a modification of the system of popular electorate founded on the principle of electoral colleges.

You see it was merely a suggestion thrown out for the Government of India, not a direction of the Medes and Persians stamp. You say:

> That for the purpose of electing members to the Provincial Councils, electoral colleges should be constituted on lines suggested by his Lordship composed exclusively of Mahomedans whose numbers and mode of grouping should be fixed by executive authority.

This comes within the principle of my despatch, and we shall see—I hope very speedily—whether the Government of India disclose objections to its practicability. Mark, electoral colleges constituted on lines "composed exclusively of Mahomedans whose members and mode of grouping should be fixed by executive authority"—that is a proposition which is not outside the despatch, but whether practicable or not is a matter for discussion between us here and the Government in India.

WHAT IS THE ALTERNATIVE?

The aim of the Government and yours is identical—that there shall be (to quote Mr. Ameer Ali's words) "adequate, real, and genuine Mahomedan representation." Now, where is the difference between us? The machinery we commended you do not think possible. What machinery? Mixed electoral colleges. Well, as I have told you, the language of the despatch does not insist upon a mixed electoral college. It would be no departure in substance from the principle of our suggestion that there should be a separate Mahomedan electorate—an electorate exclusively Mahomedan; and in view of the wide and remote distances, and difficulties of organisation, in consequence of those distances in the area constituting a large province, I am not sure that this is not one of those cases where election by two stages would not be in the highest degree convenient, and so there might be a separate electoral college exclusively Mahomedan. That is, I take it, in accordance with your own proposal. I do not commit myself to it off-hand, but thinking it very carefully over with experts, a proposal of that kind—an exclusively Mahomedan electorate sending their votes to an exclusively Mahomedan electoral college for the purpose of choosing a representative to sit in the Provincial Legislative Council—is not outside the despatch; and we shall see what view the Government of India take up on a proposal of that sort. There are various methods by which it could be done. In the first place, an election exclusively Mahomedan might be direct into the Legislative Council. The electorate might vote for a man to sit in the Legislative Council. I fancy that would be impossible by reason of distance. In the second place, you could have an election by separate communities to a local board, and the local board should be the electoral college, the Mahomedans separating themselves from the other members of the board for that purpose. Thirdly, the members of the local board, the communities being separate in the same way, could return a member for the electoral college. Fourthly, you might have a direct election to an electoral college by the community, and this electoral college would return a representative to the Legislative Council. These, you see, are four different expedients which will deserve consideration for attaining the end, having a more or less direct vote, and an exclusively Mahomedan voice in returning Mahomedan representatives.

THE BALANCE OF PARTIES.

I go to the next point, the apprehensions lest if we based our system on numerical strength alone a great injustice would be done to your community. Of course, we all considered that from the Viceroy downwards—and whether your apprehensions are well-founded or not, it is the business of those who call themselves statesmen to take those apprehensions into account and to do the best we can in setting up a great working system to allay and meet those apprehensions. (*Hear, hear.*) If you take numerical strength as your basis, in the Punjab and Eastern Bengal, Mahomedans are in a decisive majority. In the Punjab, the Moslem population is 53 per cent to 38 per cent. Hindu. In Eastern Bengal, 58 per cent. are Moslems, and 37 per cent. are Hindus. Therefore, in these two provinces, on the numerical basis alone, the Mahomedans will secure sufficient representation. In Madras, on the other hand, the Hindus are 89 per cent. against 6 per cent. of Moslems, and therefore, numbers would give no adequate representation to Moslem opinion—in fact, no representation at all. In Bombay, the Moslems are in the ratio of 3¾ to 14 millions—20 per cent. to 77 per cent. The conditions are very complex in Bombay, and I need not labour the details of this complexity. I am inclined to agree with those who think that it might be left to the local Government, either with the assent of the Central Government or otherwise, to take other elements into view required or suggested by local conditions. Coming to the United Provinces, there the Moslems are 6¾ millions to 40¾ Hindus—14 per cent. to 85 per cent. This ratio of numercial strength no more represents the proportion in elements of weight and importance than in Eastern Bengal does the Hindu ratio of 37 per cent. to 58 per cent. of Moslems. You may set off each of those two cases against the other. Then there is the great province of Bengal, where the Moslems are one quarter of the Hindus—9 millions to 39 millions—18 per cent. to 77 per cent. I do not know, but the case of Bengal deserves its own consideration.

THE PROBLEM FOR SOLUTION.

We all see, then, that this problem presents enormous difficulty—how are you going in a case like the United Provinces, for example, to secure that adequate and substantial representation which it is the interest and the desire of the Government for its own sake to have, in order that it might be rightly acquainted with the views and wishes of those for whom it is making and administering laws? No fair-minded Moslem would deny in Eastern Bengal, any more than a fair-minded non-Moslem would deny it in the United Provinces, that this is a great difficulty. You see, gentlemen, I do not despair of finding a fair-minded man in a controversy of this kind. From information that reaches me I do not at all despair of meeting fair-minded critics of both communities in spite of the very sharp antagonism which exist on many matters between them. But, whatever may be the case with Mahomedans and Hindus, there is one body of men who are bound to keep a fair mind and that is the Government. The Government are bound, whatever you may do among yourselves, strictly and I will even say sternly, to keep a fair mind and to deal with this problem in that spirit. Now, what is the object of the Government? It is that these Legislative Councils should represent truly and effectively, with a reasonable approach to the balance of real social forces, the wishes and needs of the communities themselves. That is the object of the Government, and in face of a great problem of that kind algebra, arithmetic, geometry, logic—none of these things will do your business for you. You have to look at it widely and away from those sciences, which are excellent in their place, but not always when you are solving profound complex political difficulties. I think if you allow some method of leaving to a local authority the power of adding to the number of representatives from the Mahomedan community, or the Hindu community, as the case may be, that might be a possible and prudent way of getting through this difficulty. Let us all be clear of one thing, namely—and I thought of this when I heard one or two observations that fell from Mr. Ameer Ali—that no general proposition can be wisely based on the possession of one community either of superior civil qualities or superior personal claims. If you begin to introduce that element, you can see in a moment the perils to that peace and mutual goodwill which we hope to emerge by-and-by, though it may be longer than I think. You cannot imagine anything more perilous to that peace and goodwill than a position of that kind. I repeat that I see no harm from the point of view of a practical working compromise in the principle that population, numerical strength, should be the main factor in determining how many representatives should sit for this or the other community; but modifying influences may be taken into account in allotting the numbers of such representatives.

INDIANS ON THE EXECUTIVE COUNCILS.

As regards Indian Members on the Executive Councils, if you will allow me to say so, I think it was dubious tactics to have brought that question forward. We were told by those who object, for instance, to recommend to the Crown an Indian Member of the Viceroy's Executive—we were told that it will never do, that if you put a man of one community in the other will demand a second.' Well, those who desire a recommendation of that sort to be made to the Crown certainly will not have their path made any more easy for them by this kind of manifestation. But, as it has been mentioned I should like to speak quite plainly and frankly. The Executive Council in all—this will not be in the Bill—consists of six members. Suppose there were to be two vacancies, and I were to recommend to the Crown the appointment of one Mahomedan and one Hindu, the effect would be that of the six gentlemen one-third would be non-English. That may be all right, but it would be a very serious step. Suppose you say you will bring in a Bill then. That is much more easily said than done. I am talking perfectly plainly. You would not get such a Bill. I want to talk a little more plainly. I want to say that reference to the Hindu Community or the Mahomedan community in respect to the position of the Viceroy's Executive is entirely wide of the mark in the view, I know, both of Viceroy and of myself. It is not the principle upon which a representation of this kind will be made—certainly not by me so long as I hold the office of Secretary of State, and I am perfectly sure it will not be approved by his Excellency. If, as I have already said I expect, it may be my duty by-and-by to recommend to the Crown the name of an Indian member, it will not be for a moment for the sake of placing on the Viceroy's Executive Council an Indian member simply as either a Hindu or a Mahomedan.

Decidedly we are of opinion that the Governor-General in Council will be all the more likely to transact business wisely if he has a responsible Indian adviser at his elbow. But the principle in making such a recommendation to the Crown would be to remove the apparent disability in practice—for there is no disability in law—of an Indian holding a certain appointment because he is an Indian. That is a principle we do not accept; and the principal I should go upon myself—and I know Lord Minto would say exactly the same—is the desirability of demonstrating that we hold to the famous promise made in the Proclamation of Queen Victoria in 1858, that if a man is fully qualified in proved ability and character to fill a certain post, he shall not be shut out by race or religious faith. That is our principle and beyond that I, for one, shall not be induced to go. There is a very great deal more to be said on this most important subject; but to-day I need only tell you—which I do with all respect, without complaining of what you have said, and without denying that in practical usage some day there may be means of alteration for meeting your difficulty—I do not know, I have no right to bind some one else who may fill my post—I see no chance whatever of our being able to comply with your present request.

CONCLUSION.

I have endeavoured to meet you as fairly as I possibly could. I assure you we are acting in earnest, with zeal and entire good faith; and my suggestion that any member of the Government, either in this office or the Government of India, has any prejudice whatever against Mahomedans for the purposes of political administration in India; is one of the idlest and most wicked misapprehensions that could possibly enter even into the political mind. I am greatly encouraged by having met you. I am sure that you speak in the name of important bodies of your own countrymen and of your own community: I am sure that you are going to look at our proposals in a fair and reasonable spirit, and that you are giving us credit for a desire to do the best that we possibly can in the interests of all the communities in India, including also the interests of the British Government. I can only tell you further, if you will take it from me, that if this action of the present Government—His Majesty's Government, the Government of India—fails and miscarries, and is wrecked, it will be a considerable time before another opportunity occurs. You will never again—I do not care whether the time be long or be short—you will never again have the combination of a Viceroy and a Secretary of State who are more thoroughly in earnest in their desire to improve Indian government, and to do full justice to all bodies of the Indian population.

THE INDIAN CIVIL SERVICE PROBATIONERS.

[*The Vice-Chancellor of Oxford University and the teachers of the Indian Civil Service probationers gave a dinner to the probationers on Saturday (June* 12,1909) *at the New Masonic Hall, Oxford, to meet Lord Morley of Blackburn, Secretary of State for India. The Vice-Chancellor (Dr. Warren, President of Magdalen) was in the Chair, and Sir Ernest Trevelyan was among those present.*]

Lord Morley, in proposing the toast of "The Civil Service of India," said:—Gentlemen, it is a great honour that it should fall to me to be the first Secretary of State to address this body of probationers and others. Personally, I am always delighted at any reason, good or bad, that brings me to Oxford. (*Cheers.*) A great deal of Cherwell water has flowed under Magdalen Bridge since I was an undergraduate, and even a graduate here, and I have a kind of feeling of nostalgia, which is an honourable feeling after all, when I come to Oxford. The reminiscences of one's younger days—I do not want to discourage you, quite the contrary—are apt to have in older times an ironical tinge, but that is not for any of you to-day to consider. I am glad to know that of the 50 old members of the Civil Service who are going out this autumn not less than half are Oxford men, most of them, nearly all of them, Oxford bred, and even the three or four who are not Oxford bred are practically, so far as can be, Oxford men. Now I will go a little wider. An Indian Minister is rather isolated in the public eye amid the press and bustle of the political energies, perplexities, interests, and partisan passions that stir and concentrate attention on our own home affairs. Yet let me assure you that there is no ordinary compensation for that isolation in the breast of an Indian Minister. He finds that compensation in the enormous magnitude and the endless variety of all the vast field of interests, present and still more future, that are committed to his temporary charge. Though his charge may be temporary, I should think every Secretary of State remembers that even in that fugitive span of his days he may do either some good or, if he is unhappy, he may do some harm.

ENGLAND'S ONLY REAL EMPIRE.

This week London has been enormously excited by the Imperial Press Conference, and I was excited too. (*Laughter.*) But I was rather struck by the extraordinarily small attention, almost amounting to nothing, that was given to the Dominion that you here are concerned with. No doubt an Imperial Conference raises one or two very delicate questions as to whether common citizenship is to be observed or whether the relations between India, for example, and the Colonies should remain what they are. Well, I am not going to expatiate upon that to-night, but it did occur to me in reading all these proceedings that the part of Hamlet was rather omitted, because India, after all, is the only real Empire. You there have an immense Dominion, an almost countless population, governed by foreign rulers—and that is what an Empire is. However, I will not go into that to-night, but I observed it all with a rather grim feeling in my mind that, if anything goes wrong in India, the whole of what we are talking about now, the material and military conditions of the Empire as a whole, might be strangely altered. Now, one of the happy qualities of youth—and there is no pleasure greater than to see you for those who have passed beyond that stage—is not to be, I think I am right, in a hurry, not to be too anxious either for the present or future measure or the responsibilities of life and a career. You will forgive me if I remind you of what I am sure you all know—that the civil government of 230,000,000 persons in British India is in the hands of some 1,200 men who belong to the Indian Civil Service. Now, let us follow that. Any member of a body so small must be rapidly placed in a position of command, and it is almost startling to me, when I look round on the fresh physiognomies of those who have returned (*laughter*), to think of the contrast between the position, we will say, of some of your Oxford contemporaries who are lawyers and who have to spend, many of them, a good many years possibly in chambers in Lincoln's Inn or the Temple waiting for briefs that do not come. Contrast your position with that of members who enter the Home

Civil Service, an admirable service; but still, for a good long time, a member who enters that service has got to pursue the minor and slightly mechanical routine of Whitehall. (*Laughter.*) You will not misunderstand me, because nobody knows better than a Minister how tremendous is the debt he owes to the permanent officials of his department. Certainly, I am the last man to under-rate that. Well, now, any of you may be rapidly placed in a position of real command with enormous responsibilities. I am speaking in the presence of men who know better than I do all the details of this, but it is true that one of you in a few years may be placed in command of a district and have 1,000,000 human beings committed to his charge. He may have to deal with a famine; he may have to deal with a riot; he may take a decision on which the lives of thousands of people may depend. Well, I think that early call to responsibility, to a display of energy, to the exercise of individual decision and judgment is what makes the Indian Civil Service a fine career. (*Cheers.*) And that is what has produced an extraordinary proportion of remarkable men in that great service. I cannot imagine a career richer in occasions which call out these qualities.

THE INDIAN CIVIL SERVICE AS A CAREER.

There is another elevating thought that I should suppose is present to all of you, to those who are already in important posts and those who are by-and-by going to take them up. The good name of England is in your keeping. (*Cheers.*) Your conduct and the conduct of your colleagues in other branches of the Indian Service decides what these people of India are to think of British Government and of those who represent it. Of course, you cannot expect the simple villager to care anything or to know anything about the abstraction called the *raj*. What he knows is the particular officer who stands in front of him and with whom he has dealings. If that officer is harsh or overbearing or incompetent, the Government gets the discredit of it; he assumes the Government is also harsh, overbearing, and incompetent. There is this peculiarity which strikes me about the Indian Civil Servant. I am not sure that all of you will at once welcome it, but it goes to the root of the matter. He is always more or less on duty. It is not merely when he is doing his office work, but he is always more or less on duty, and the great men of that great service have always recognised this obligation, that official relations are not to be the beginning and the end of the duties of an Indian administrator. It has been my pleasure and privilege during the three or four years I have been at the India Office to see a stream of important Indian officials come round home by my office, and I gather from them that one of the worst drawbacks of the modern speeding-up of the great wheels of the machine of Indian Government is that the Indian Civil Servant has less time and less opportunity than he used to have of bringing himself into close contact with those with whose interests he is concerned. One of these important officials told me the other day this story: A retired veteran, an Indian soldier of some kind or another, had come to him and said:

> This is an odd state of things. The other day so-and-so, a young commissioner or what not, was coming down to my village or district. We did the best we could to get a good camping-ground for him. He arrived with his attendants. He went into his tent. He immediately began to write. He went on writing. We thought he had got very urgent business to do. We went away. We arrived in the morning soon after dawn. He was still writing, or he had begun again, and so concerned was he both in the evening and in the morning with his writing that we really had nothing from him but a polite salaam.

This was told to me by an important official, and it may or may not be typical, but I can imagine it is possible, at all events. That must be pure mischief. If I am going to remain Indian Secretary, I was going to say for a dozen years to come, certainly my efforts would be devoted to an abatement of that enormous amount of writing. (*Cheers.*) You applaud that sentiment now, but you will applaud it more by-and-by.

SOCIAL RELATIONS WITH INDIANS.

But upon this point of less time being devoted to writing and more time to cultivating social relations with the people, it is very easy for us here, no doubt, to say you ought to cultivate social relations, but I can imagine a man who has done a hard day's office work—I am sure I should feel it myself—is not inclined to launch out upon talk and enquiries and so forth among the people with whom he is immediately concerned. I can imagine it is asking almost in a way too much from human nature. Still, that is the thing to aim at—not exacting too much from human nature. The thing to aim at is—all civilians who write and speak say the same—to cultivate social relations so far as you can. I do not mean in the towns, I am rather sceptical from my observation of them, but in the local communities with which many of you are going to be concerned. It seems to me that much might be done in that way. I saw the other day a letter from a lady, not, I fancy, particularly sentimental about this matter, and she said this:—

> There would be great improvement if only better social relations could be established with Indians personally. I do wish that all young officials could be primed before they came out with the proper ideas on this question.

Well, I have no illusions whatever as to my right or power of priming you. I think each of us can see for himself the desirability of every one who goes out there having certain ideas in his head as to his own relations with the people whom he is called upon to govern. That is the mission with which we have to charge you, and it is as momentous a mission as was ever confided to any great military commander or any admiral—this mission of yours to place yourselves in touch with the people whom you have got to govern. I am under no illusions that I can plant new ideas in your minds compared with the ideas that may be planted by experienced heads of Indian Government. The other day I saw a letter of instructions from a very eminent Lieutenant-Governor to those of the next stage below him as to the attitude that they were to take to the new civilians when they arrived, and you 24 or 25 gentlemen will get the benefit of those instructions if you are going to that province. I do not think there is any reason why I should not mention his name—it was Sir Andrew Fraser, the retired Lieutenant-Governor of Bengal—and those instructions as to the temper that was to be inculcated upon newcomers were marked by a force, a fulness, and a first-hand aptitude which not even the keenest Secretary of State could venture to approach. I know that exile is hard. It is very easy for us here to preach. Exile is and must be hard, but I feel confident that under the guidance of the great officials there under whom you will find yourselves, you will take care not to ignore the Indian; not to hold apart and aloof from the Indian life and ways, not to believe that you will not learn anything by conversation with educated Indians. (*Cheers.*) And while you are in India and among Indians and responsible to Indians, because you are as responsible to them as you are to us here, while you are in that position, gentlemen, do not live in Europe all the time. (*Cheers.*) Whether or not—I am quite candid—it was a blessing either for India or for Great Britain that this great responsibility fell upon us, whatever the ultimate destiny and end of all this is to be, at any rate I for my part know of no more imposing and momentous transaction than the Government of India by you and those like you. I know of no more imposing and momentous transaction in the vast scroll of the history of human Government. (*Cheers.*)

PAST DIFFICULTIES AND PRESENT PROSPECTS.

We have been within the last two years in a position of considerable difficulty. But the difficulties of

Indian Government are not the result—be sure of this —of any single incident or set of incidents. You see it said that all the present difficulties arise from the Partition of Bengal, but I have never believed that. I do not think well of that operation, but that does not matter. I was turning the other day to the history of the Oxford Mission to Calcutta. In 1899—the Partition of Bengal, as you know, was much later—what did they say? "There exists at present."—at present in 1899—"an increasing hostility to what is European and English among the educated classes." "No one can have," this Oxford report goes on, "any real knowledge of India without a deep sense of the splendid work done by the great Indian Civil Service—the finest service the world has ever seen." (*Cheers.*) "The work is recognised by the Indian people. They thoroughly appreciate the benefits of our rule, they are bound to us by self-interest, but they do not like us." However that may be, we shall see. It is intelligible, but that is a result to be carefully guarded against by demeanour, by temper, by action—to be guarded against at every turn. I think every one would agree that anything like a permanent estrangement between the Indians and the Europeans would be a dire failure and a most tremendous catastrophe. Well, I am coming to other grounds. The history of the last six months has been important and anxious and trying. Eight months ago there certainly was severe tension. Now, that tension has relaxed, and the great responsible officials on the spot assure me that the position of the hour and the prospects are reassuring. We—that is to say, the Government of India and the Secretary of State in Council—have kept the word which was given by the Sovereign on November 1, last year, in the message to the people of India, commemorating the fiftieth anniversary of the assumption of the powers of Government in India by the Crown—the transfer of the power from the old Company to the Crown. We have kept our word. We have introduced and carried through Parliament a measure, every body will admit of the highest importance, a measure for certain degrees of reconstitution that was carried through both Houses with excellent deliberation. I have been in Parliament a great many years. I have never known a measure discussed and conducted with such a knowledge and such a desire to avoid small, petty, personal incidents. I have never known a measure conducted through Parliament in a way more worthy of the reputation of Parliament. (*Cheers.*)

A "STAGE OF INTENSE INTEREST."

Well, now, you are entering upon your duties at a stage of intense interest. I saw something Sir Charles Elliot, who was Lieutenant-Governor of Bengal, had written the other day, and he says this is "the most momentous change ever effected by Parliament in the Constitution of the Government of India since 1858." He goes on to say that no prudent man would prophesy. No, and I do not prophesy. How could I? It depends upon two things: It depends, first of all, upon the Civil Service;

no, I think I will not divide them. It depends on the Civil Service and it depends on the power of Indians with the sense and instincts of Government to control the wilder and more childish spirits with neither the sense nor the instincts of Government. As for the Civil Service, which is the other branch on which all depends, it is impossible not to be struck with the warmest admiration of the loyal and manful tone in which leading members of the Civil Service have expressed their resolution to face the new tasks that this new legislation will impose upon them. I have not got it with me now, I wish I had; but certain language was used by Sir Norman Baker, who is now the Lieutenant-Governor of Bengal. I think I quoted it in the House of Lords and, if I could read it to you, it would be far better than any speech of mine in support of the toast I am going to propose to you. There never was a more manful and admirable expression of the devotion of the great service than the promise of their cordial, whole-hearted, and laborious support of the policy which they have now got to carry through. I am certain there is not one of you who will fall short, and I am speaking in the presence of those who are not probationers, but persons proved. There is not one of you who, when the time comes, will not respond to the call in the same spirit in which Sir Norman Baker responded. I am now going to take you, if you will allow me, for a moment to a point of immediate and, I can almost say, personal interest. Everybody will agree, as I say, that we have fulfilled within the last six or eight months the pledges that were given by the Sovereign in November. (*Cheers.*) An Indian gentleman has been placed on the Council of the Viceroy—not an every-day transaction. It needed some courage; it was done. Before that two Indians were placed on the Council of India that sits in my own office at Whitehall. We have passed through Parliament, as I have already described to you, this great measure.

MR. MACKARNESS "VOTE OF CENSURE."

Those are great things; that is a great operation: But then I am told there is great uneasiness growing in the House of Commons as to the matter of deportation, you know what deportation means. It means that nine Indian gentlemen on December 13 last were arrested and are now detained—arrested under a law which is as good a law as any law on our own Statute Book. You will forgive me for detaining you with this, but it is rather an actual and pressing point. Some of the most respected members of my own party write a letter to the Prime Minister protesting. A Bill has been brought in and the first reading of it was carried two or three days ago, of which I can only say—with all responsibility for what I am saying—that it is nothing less, if you consider the source from which it is supported, than a vote of censure on me and Lord Minto. The Bill is supported by a very clever and very rising and perfectly honourable member of the Opposition also. Now words of an extraordinary character have been used in support of this severe criticism of the policy of myself and Lord Minto. In a motion, not in connection with the Bill, but earlier in the session, words were read from Magna Charta, with the insinuation that the present Secretary of State is as dubious a character as the Sovereign against whom Magna Charta was directed. (*Laughter.*) Gloomy references were made to King Charles I, and it was shown that we were exercising powers that led, when attempted to be exercised by Charles I, to the Civil War that cost Charles I, his head. (*Laughter.*) This was at the beginning of the present session. I doubt if they will get through to the end of the session, whenever that may be, without comparisons being instituted between the Secretary of State, for example, and Strafford, or even Cromwell in his worst moments, as they would think. Well, if Cromwell is mentioned I think. I shall know where to point out how Cromwell was troubled by Fifth Monarchy men, Praise-God Barebones, Venner, Saxby, and others. In historical parallels I am really fairly prepared. (*Laughter.*) I will try my chance, at all events.

AN "EMERGENCY POWER" AGAINST "EVIL-DOERS."

Now, let us look at this really seriously, because really serious minds are exercised by deportation. On December 13, nine Indians were arrested under a certain Indian regulation of the year 1818, and they who reproach us with violating 1215, which is Magna Charta, and the Petition of Rights, complain that 1818 is far too remote for us to be at all affected by anything that was then made law. Now, what is the regulation? I will ask you to follow me pretty closely only for a minute or two. The regulation of 1818 says:—

> Reasons of State occasionally render it necessary to place under personal restraint individuals against whom there may not be sufficient grounds to institute any judicial proceedings, and the Governor-General in Council is able for good and sufficient reasons to determine that A. B.—whoever he may be—shall be placed under personal restraint.

Let us face that. There is no trial; there is no charge; there is no fixed limit of time of detention; and, in short, it is equivalent, no doubt, to a suspension of *Habeas Corpus*. That is a broad statement, but substantially that is what it is. Now, I do not deny for a moment that if proceedings of this kind, such as took place on December 13 last year, were normal or frequent, if they took place every day of the week or every week of the month, it would be dangerous and in the highest degree discreditable to our whole government in India. It would be detestable and dangerous, but is there to be no such thing as an emergency power? I am not talking about England, Scotland, or Ireland. I am talking about India. Is there to be no such thing as an emergency power? My view is that the powers given under the regulation of 1818 do constitute an emergency power which may be lawfully applied if there be an emergency. Was there an emergency last December? I will tell you. The Government of India found in December a movement which was a grave menace to the very foundations of public peace and security. The list of crimes for 12 months was formidable showing the determined and daring character of the supporters of this movement. The crimes were not all. Terrorism prevented evidence. The ordinary process of law was no longer adequate, and the impression in this community, in which you are all going to take your part, was that the Government could be defied with impunity. Well, the Government of India did not need to pass a new law. We found in the armoury of weapons of Government a law, and applied it. Very disagreeable, but still we should have been perfectly unworthy of holding the position we do—I am speaking now of the Government of India and myself—if we had not taken that weapon out of the armoury and used it against these evil-doers. (*Cheers.*)

NOT CONDEMNED BY INDIAN OPINION.

It was vital that we should stamp out this impression that the Government of India could be defied with impunity, not in matters of opinion, but in matters affecting peace, order, life and property—that the Government in those elementary conditions of social existence could be defied with impunity. I say, then—I may be misunderstood, but I will say it all the same—it was especially vital in that week of December that these severe proceedings should be taken if there was to be any fair and reasonable chance for those reforms which have since come to a birth, which had been for very many months upon the anvil, and to which we looked, as we look now, for a real pacification. It was not the first time that this arbitrary power—for it is that, I never disguise it—was used. It was used some years ago—I forget how many. I was talking the other day to an officer who was greatly concerned in it in Poona, and he described the conditions, and told me the effect was magical. I do not say the effect of our proceedings the other day was magical. At all events, bombs and knives and pistols and so forth are not at an end. None of the great officers in India thinks that we may not have some of these over again, but at any rate for the moment, and, I believe, for much more than the moment, we have secured order and tranquillity and acquiescence, and a warm approval of and interest in our reforms. I have said we have had acceptance of our reforms. What a curious thing it is that, after the reforms were announced and after the deportations had taken place, still there came to Lord Minto deputations, and to me many telegrams, conveying their appreciation and gratitude for the reforms, for all those things we have done. Some of our good friends should move what is in effect a vote of censure upon us. They are better Indians than the Indians themselves. (*Laughter.*) I cannot imagine a more mistaken proceeding.

A FINAL WORD.

Now let me say one more word about the deportations. It is true that there is no definite charge that could be produced in a court of law. That is the very essence of the whole transaction. Then it is said:—" Oh, but you look to the police; you get all your evidence from the police." That is not so. The Government of India get their information, not evidence in a technical sense—that is the root of the matter—from important district officers. But it is said then: "Who is to decide the value of the information?" I heard that one gentleman in the House of Commons said privately in ordinary talk: "If English country gentlemen were to decide this, we would not mind." Who do decide? Do you think this is done by a police-sergeant in a box? On the contrary, every one of these nine cases of deportation has been examined and investigated—by whom? By Lord Minto, by the late Lieutenant-Governor of Bengal, by the present Lieutenant-Governor of Bengal, by two or three members of the Viceroy's Council. Come, are we to suppose for a minute that men of this great station and authority and responsibility are going to issue a *lettre de cachet* for A.B., C.D., or E.F., without troubling themselves whether that *lettre de cachet* is wisely issued or not? It is absurd to lay any stress whatever upon that point. Well, then, it is said of a man who is arrested, not on a charge, not on a conviction of a court: "Oh, he ought not to be harshly treated." He is not harshly treated. If he is one of these nine deported men, he is not put into contact with criminal persons. His family are looked after. He subsists under conditions which are to an Indian perfectly conformable to his social position and to the ordinary comforts and conveniences of his life. The greatest difference is drawn between these nine men and other men against whom charges to be judicially tried are brought. The last observation I have to make is that all these cases will come up for periodic reconsideration. They will come up very shortly, and that consideration will be conducted with a great regard naturally for justice, for firmness, for steadfastness, and for resolution. There will be no attempt at all to look at this transaction of these nine deported men otherwise than as a disagreeable measure, but as a measure imposed upon us by a sense of public duty and a measure that events justify, because let us just remember this that, while Lord Minto and I are to have a vote of censure, covert or direct, the Indians send their deputations to us. What did Mr. Gokhale, who is a leader of a considerable body of important political opinion in India, say? Did he move a vote of censure? He said in the Legislative Council the other day in Calcutta that Lord Minto and the Secretary of State had saved India from drifting into chaos. Therefore, to end that matter, I think we shall withstand our enemies in the gate with a clear gaze, to borrow the King's expression as to our whole system for 50 years. We shall face it with a clear gaze and a good conscience. (*Cheers.*) I owe you an apology for pressing Parliamentary points upon your attention, but they are important, and I am glad you have allowed me to say what I have said of them. I invite you now to drink the health of "The Civil Service of India."

THE MONTAGU REFORMS.

[*Viscount Morley emerged from his retirement on Thursday July 25, 1918 at the National Liberal Club, London, to receive a whole hearted tribute from Indian admirers. When Sir Krishna Gupta retired from the India Council, he and a number of distinguished compatriots formed a Committee for the presentation of his bust, in marble, to Lord Morley. The artist selected was Mr. Bruce Joy, and the result of his labours was presented to Lord Morley on behalf of ' his Indian admirers in grateful recognition of his enlightened and far-sighted statesmanship and his invaluable services to the people of India while Secretary of State.' In turn, Lord Morley, as a convinced ' National Liberal,' presented the bust to the National Liberal Club, which has given it the place of honour in the entrance hall. The bust was unveiled by Lady Baig. Lord Morley said in reply :—*]

HE recognized the touching significance of the feeling which had prompted the selection of this particular symbol of goodwill and affectionate friendship. Referring to his official life in connection with India, he said that he deeply regretted the absence of Lord Minto, who was Viceroy during his term of office as Secretary of State and who was the most loyal comrade and the most admirable of fellow-workers. He (Lord Morley) could never have gone on but for the steady and prudent support given to him by the late Mr. Gokhale.

The motto of Lord minto and himself was 'Rally the moderates,' and he hoped that that would continue to be the aim whatever changes might be necessary, no security could be certain unless they had the moderates with them. Lord Minto once wrote to him, 'I do believe we can accumulate great influence if we only give to the people of India evidence of sympathy.' Then the present Sovereign of this realm, who had just returned from India, made a speech at the Guildhall in which he said that sympathy was the keyword to success in holding the loyalty of and doing service for the Indians. Sympathy was no substitute for wise government; but, on the other hand, no Government was wise which tried to do without it, and that certainly was a maxim that was followed during the time that Lord Minto was responsible for the Government of India.

Lord Cromer had said a wise thing when he declared that it was much better to give an Indian an appointment over an Englishman, even though he was the less competent of the two. That was paradoxical, but it meant that you gained more in popular content than you lost in not having the best administrator. Neither Lord Minto nor he ever claimed genius of Aristotle; they were not great jurists, and otherwise they were inferior to Aristotle. One did not need to have the genius of Aristotle to perceive that a Viceroy and Secretary of State would be all the more likely to understand the feeling, the opinions, the drift of India if they had an Indian on the Advisory Executive Council. Looking back upon that controversy, he would say that the most essential of all reforms was the adoption of the principle that no Indian was unfitted as such to fulfil the highest duties of citizenship and the highest responsibilities of government. He recalled in this connexion the solemn and sacred promise given by Queen Victoria that membership of any race within the Empire should not disqualify for the holding of office.

The admission of an Indian to the Secretary of State's Council was the most stiffly opposed of all the Morley-Minto reforms, but it was now the one reform to which there was no opposition at all. It had been, on the contrary, extended and amplified. In this respect they had been thoroughly justified by experience.

THE REFORMS.

Not being in the list of the millenarians, neither Lord Minto nor himself ever said that their reforms would put a stop to agitation, or that they would satisfy the political hunger of India. He was content, and he was sure Lord Minto would have been content, when he read that the feeling of the people of India was never so good as in 1914. Lord Hardinge also spoke of the vast political improvement that had taken place, and said it was entirely due to Lord Minto and himself.

It was a great misfortune, he proceeded, when a country was overtaken by the rage for experiment. In Indian waters they could only proceed by constant, regular heaving of the lead—by trying to find some middle way between the half-truth of bold political enterprise and the half-truth of political timidity.

Correspondents had asked him what he thought of the proposed reforms. He would be precipitate if he gave a bold 'Aye' or 'No' of praise or dispraise, though it would not matter if he did. He had given a careful study to the Report ('Copiousness' he remarked humorously,' makes everything more respectable to me; it is a literary habit') but he was not going to pronounce on the clauses, or what might happen on the committee stages and he felt that he could not be mistaken in tracing the lineaments of the the parental physiognomy of 1909 in the progeny of 1918. He had been reproached for stating that he would not take part in a reform of India that might lead to an Indian Parliament. He would like to know what was meant by a Parliament. He did not know whether the outcome of the proposals now before the country would amount to a Parliament, and what sort of a Parliament it would be. Therefore, that might well be postponed. But no one could suppose for a moment that all the convulsion and passion sweeping over the world was going to pass India by. Nothing could be more irrational than to imagine the people of India as saying that they were out of all this and wanted nothing. There were great and powerful bodies of Indians of whom that was not in the least degree true. As to the immediate proposals, he had the privilege and advantage of being the colleague of the Secretary of State for India, and while he felt that Mr. Montagu's orders were more likely to be, on the whole, recommended than any other that could be imagined, he deprecated at this early stage in the discussion the kind of truculence of tone already adopted by some organs of opinion who treated this serious and important movement in connexion with India as if it were a mere passing difference in our own public and political life. We need all the freedom from party passion that we could get to bring us safely through the difficult position in which we were. He had the highest admiration for the zealous counsels and active experience and influence which Mr. Montagu had brought to bear on the problems of Indian government from the day that he entered the India Office, and no doubt he had continually cast the lead and taken his soundings before making his recommendations. Was it surprising that India should show herself alive and awake to all the events that were known passing in the world? But while we rejoiced in the political progress that was taking place in India, let us be sure that we do not fall back into political retrogression in our own country. He would repeat a few questions put by Lord Macaulay in 1833. Lord Macaulay said:— 'Do you think we can give the Indians knowledge without awakening their ambition? Do you think we can awaken their ambition without giving them some legitimate vent for it?' And then he said:—'It may be the public mind of India may expand under our system until it has outgrown our system'—that was to say, that, having become instructed in European knowledge, the Indians might in some future age demand European institutions. That was a process, said Lord Morley, which would have to be carefully watched. It would have to be faced, and those would be just and wise statesmen who did not shrink from letting the Imperial public realize all that might lie before them. It could not be met by dogmatic negatives; there would have to be considerate treatment whether in the form of Mr. Montagu's proposals or any other form.

APPENDIX A.

THE FORWARD POLICY.

[*Mr. John Morley, M. P. addressing his constituents at Arbroath, N. B., on September* 28, 1897, *said in the course of his speech :*—]

Well, now I am going to take you to India, where, as you know, there is a conflagration of more or less magnitude upon the North-Western Frontier. I am sure you all read what goes on in these military operations. Gentlemen, this is not at all the time for opening up the large and even momentous issues which are involved in our frontier policy. Brave men and skilful men are now striving, at the peril of their lives, to bring to an end the mischief which unwise men set loose. We watch the efforts of these brave men of ours, and of their native comrades, with interest and with confidence, and we all wish them a rapid success in their unwelcome and, I venture to think, barren task. But while this is not a moment to discuss the policy, it is a moment when untoward events quicken political comprehensions, and quicken national consciences; it is a moment, while we watch this endeavour to cut down the fire, to look at the policy which kindled the flame.

THE RESULT OF THE "FORWARD" POLICY.

I am not going into it at any length, because there is one other subject which will take me all the time that your patience will permit. But I will say this, and this is clear, that this fierce rising of the wild tribes on the North-Western frontier of India is the result of the prevalence for some years past of a forward policy, and especially—and I call your attention to this—of the unfortunate determination of the present Government to follow a policy of activity in extension in the direction of the Valley of Chitral. You will recollect that in the spring of 1895, a military expedition was despatched to rescue certain British Officers in danger at Chitral. The rescue was effected with remarkable promptitude and energy, and then the question was left whether we should retain a foothold in Chitral or keep away. That came before the Liberal Cabinet of 1895. The Government of India held the view that we ought to hold on; men, on the other hand, of the highest military authority and experience were adverse. They said: "You had much better come away," and so far as we, the Government of 1895, were able to ascertain, the preponderance of expert and valuable military opinion was in favour of our coming away. I won't detain you with talking as to general grounds, financial grounds, and otherwise, which were present before us, but I cannot pass over one of the most important of all the considerations that were present in our minds when we determined on the evacuation of Chitral. When the expedition was setting out for the relief of Dr. Robertson, the Viceroy issued a proclamation—and I would invite your serious attention to this because your judgment on transactions of this kind goes to the roots of national honour and national character. The Viceroy issued a proclamation in which he promised certain tribes that the Government had no intention of permanently occupying any territories through which a certain chief's misconduct might now force them to pass, or of interfering with the independence of the tribes, and that as soon as the particular object with which they entered Chitral territory had been obtained, the force would be withdrawn. It was because of that promise of the Viceroy that some of these wild tribesmen allowed the forces of the Indian Government to go through their territory. We held that to take any step which might be construed as meaning a permanent occupation of the Chitral Valley, or of the territory of the tribesmen, would be to break faith—and to break faith, mark you, as I have already said with those who, on the strength of this promise, had not opposed the advance of our relief expedition. Well, we decided in 1895 to direct the evacuation of the Chitral territory. Events have proved that we were terribly right. (*Cheers.*) On the very day on which my able and eloquent friend, who was then Secretary for India, Sir Henry Fowler, was sitting down to write his despatch conveying this decision, I think that was the very day when an adverse vote in the House of Commons unfortunately slit the thread of our existence. What happened afterwards was that our successors, in the plenitude of their wisdom and their foresight, flung themselves into the arms of the forward party, of the military party, with the lamentable results you see. I do not deny that other causes contributed to this outbreak, but no reasonable man can or does doubt that the non-fulfilment of our promise had a powerful effect in stirring up the frontier tribes against us. There was a regular course only too familiar to us in all these forward operations.

THE "FORWARD" RAKE'S PROGRESS.

These are the five stages of the "forward" Rake's progress. (*Laughter.*) First, to push on into places where you have no business to be, and where you had promised you would not go—(*hear, hear*)—second, your intrusion is resented, and in these wilds resentment means resistance; third, you instantly cry out that the people are rebels and their act is rebellion, in spite of your own assurances that you had no intention of setting up a permanent sovereignty over them; fourth, you send forces to stamp out the rebellion; fifth, having spread bloodshed and confusion and anarchy, you declare with hands uplifted to heaven, that moral reasons force you to say, for if you were to leave, this territory would be left in a condition no civilised power could contemplate with equanimity and composure. These are the five stages of the "forward" Rake's progress.

THE GOVERNMENT'S WANT OF FORESIGHT.

To show how blind these men are, let me recall what the Secretary of State for India, when declining this section in 1895, said of this operation, after this reversal of our policy? "We have now arrived"—this is two years ago—" at a settlement of our frontier difficulties. We have, I think, by these arrangements, utilised the results of the Chitral expedition, and my one wish now is"—that is the Secretary of State speaking in 1895—"to look to the condition of Indian finance, to associate with the satisfactory settlement of these frontier questions a period of quietude and economy." *(Laughter.)* That was the degree of foresight of Her Majesty's Government. Was there ever so unlucky a prophet? "A satisfactory settlement of these frontier questions." You see how they are settled. "Quietude and economy!" Why, I am told by those who are very competent to judge these proceedings that they will cost five millions sterling if they cost a rupee. "Quietude and economy! This is all I have to say on this point. There will be much to be said about it before we have done with it. It is obviously bad to turn these tribes into enemies, and to incline them to be the friends of the invader, if ever an invader should be minded to approach India through those high uplands and valleys. It is bad, but what is worst of all is that it means laying upon India which is a poor country, and which is at this moment in vast areas undergoing all the horrors and distress of famine—it means imposing upon India a burden which India cannot reasonably, perhaps, not possibly, be expected to bear. From my point of view the military side is the least part of this unfortunate proceeding—it is the effect upon Indian finance. Many men of the highest authority will tell you that the finance of India, even as it is, is a ruinous finance. I won't argue, but I saw a statement the other day that the cost of the "forward" policy in India during the last twenty years has been something like £50,000,000 sterling. And now you will add several millions more. Gentlemen, you really think it is a far cry from Arbroath to Calcutta, but you are responsible; you in Arbroath here, though far from Calcutta and Simla, are responsible. You can protect yourselves; you have your representatives in the House of Commons and can protect yourselves partially through your representative but the Indian tax-payer is helpless and I am sure you will agree with me that it is a monstrous thing, upon a point whether military experts differ diametrically, to put upon this wretched and famine and plague-stricken country an increased burden, because some military men say that if you take this valley or that valley your frontier will be a little safe. (*"Nonsense," and laughter.*) I, for one, agree with my friend here who says it is all nonsense. Is it common sense? If there were to be Russian or any other invasion of India, is it not far better that Russia should have, or any invader should have, to make her way against hostile tribes through this intractable country and then find itself face to face with a British force that has been marching fully prepared? It does not require a General to see the folly of this policy. (*Hear, hear.*)

APPENDIX—B.

BACK TO LORD LAWRENCE.

[*The following speech was delivered on October 4, at Forfar by Mr. John Morley:*—]

You may have seen that, when I was speaking the other night in another burgh of this group, I referred to a state of affairs on the North-Western frontier of India, and I ventured to point out that the doings of the present Government as contrasted with the doings of the late Government, in the matter of what is known as Chitral, were certainly, in some part, responsible for the unpleasant conflagration which is now raging on the frontier. Well, I have been taken to book for all this by a newspaper in Scotland, which is always remarkable for the affability with which it conducts political controversy. (*Laughter, and "hear, hear.*") They say—and I think it is worth while for me to nail a bad shilling to the counter when I see it—(a *laugh and "hear, hear.*")—they say—and the subject is one of great importance—they say that, after all, Lord Kimberley, who was the Secretary of State for India in the Government of which I had the honour to be a member, said this—that it was a matter of importance that we should be able to control the external affairs of Chitral. Well, and then they ask, plausibly enough, how can you control the external affairs of Chitral if you have no post of observation there? Well, but then, up to five years ago, there was no Resident in Chitral and Lord Kimberley himself, whom they vouch as overthrowing the position which I ventured to take up at Arbroath—they forget that Lord Kimberley himself said, having alleged that we ought to maintain—that we ought to be able to control the external affairs of Chitral—that Lord Kimberley himself said it was not intended to maintain permanently a Resident Officer in Chitral. Well, I don't know. These are very technical matters, but I hope you follow them. It may be said "Oh, but since Lord Kimberley said it was not intended to retain a Resident at Chitral, there has been the campaign." Gentlemen, that does not affect the argument at all. If it was not important, as the Secretary of State of our Government said it was not, to maintain permanently a Resident in Chitral before the argument which was arrived at between Russia and ourselves in respect of the Pamirs, how on earth can it be more important now than it was then to have a Resident there—to retain a post of observation? Gentlemen, since the agreement between ourselves and Russia upon the Pamir frontier has been arrived at, whatever arguments there were before for our retention of an Agent at Chitral, have not been strengthened, but weakened by that very agreement come to between ourselves and Russia.

"ANOTHER BAD SHILLING."

Well, I must detain you for a minute more whilst I nail another bad shilling to the counter which has been attempted to be put into circulation from the same mint. Our very able friend, Sir Henry Fowler, the Secretary of State for India after Lord Kimberley, is also vouched as making it impossible for persons to make good the charge of breach of faith. And what did Sir Henry Fowler say in the House of Commons? He made two speeches in August or September, 1895, and what he said in these two speeches in the same debate came to this, that if the Government made a road through the territory of these tribes, otherwise than by peaceable arrangement with the tribes, to whom a certain proclamation was issued, then there would have been a breach of faith with these tribes. Well, is it contended—and this is almost all I have got to say on the matter—is it contended that a peaceable arrangement was made? The rising, which some of you may have read of, in the Swat Valley, was at the beginning—at all events, it happened in the early part of these troubles on the Indian frontier—and was a protest, as Indian experts inform us against the right of transit claimed by the Indian Government. Well, so much—I am not to detain you more than that—so much for the right of our political opponents to vouch the fast Liberal Secretary of State. (*Cheers.*)

THE POLICY OF LAWRENCE IS THE POLICY OF THE LIBERAL PARTY.

But I don't want quite to leave this subject. I must have another sentence on it to say. I don't want to leave it, because I believe there is nothing on which Liberals ought to set their hearts more firmly than resistance—strong resistance—to what is called the forward policy in India. (*Cheers.*) This is no new story. Those of you who are old enough to recollect well, as I do, all the talk something like twenty years ago about a scientific frontier, those arguments—the arguments of what were called a scientific frontier then, were exactly the arguments which we hear to-day, and on which we shall hear more by and by; and the same resistance which was offered to those arguments—the same dispersion of the force of those arguments in 1878-9-80—I believe the same resistance ought to be offered, and will be offered, to any further tamperings with what is called a forward policy. When I am asked as I am asked by these journals who oppose us in Scotland, why, instead of dwelling so much on the point of breach of faith why we don't declare our policy in broad terms. I am quite willing to meet them, and answer them. I am not to expound our policy in any poor terms of mine. I will expound it in the words of one of the most able, experienced and powerful Indian Governors that India has ever had. I will tell you what Lord Lawrence said. I won't give it to you in his own words, but mainly in his own words and this is what it comes to: "Should a foreign power, such as Russia, ever seriously think of invading India from without, or of stirring up the elements of disaffection or anarchy within it, our strongest security would lie in previous abstinences from entanglements at either Kabul, Kandahar, or any similar outpost. It would be in full reliance on a compact and disciplined army stationed within our own territories. It would lie—and you will well be able to understand this—in the contentment of the masses of the population of India. (*Cheers.*) It would lie in the construction of material works within British India, which enhance the comfort to the people, while they add to our political stability and strength. It would lie in husbanding our finances and consolidating and multiplying our resources. It would lie in the rectitude and honesty of our intentions coupled with the avoidance of all sources of complaint, which either invite foreign aggression or stir up restless spirits of revolt." (*Cheers.*) When you see it stated in these prints that we have no policy, my answer is, that we fall back upon that policy every step in deserting which has been accomplished by mischievous expenditure, by some political mischiefs, and every step forward from which will involve you in further expenditure, if not in more and deeper mischiefs than those mischiefs of expenditure. (*Hear, hear.*)

APPENDIX C.

THE WAR BEYOND THE INDIAN FRONTIER.

[*In the course of a speech delivered at Stirling, on January 27, 1898, the Right Hon'ble John Morley M. P., said*:—]

A few words upon the Indian frontier question. I read with the utmost amazement what the Secretary of State for the Colonies said regarding the frontier war. He expressed what I cannot but call a novel opinion, a pernicious opinion, a highly dangerous opinion, and it is this: "Would you trust," he says upon this frontier question, "would you trust the observations made by ourselves, who have to learn everything within a few months or a few years from documents and papers, or would you trust those who, like the Indian Government, have been engaged for years and years in studying this question, and the military experts whose business it is to understand and study the military aspects of the case? The late Government were prepared to override the unanimous opinions of the Indian Government and the opinions of the majority of the greatest experts in military science." First of all, and I am speaking in the presence of a confederate, as a matter of fact, it is wholly incorrect and wholly misleading. (*Hear, hear.*) Men of the highest military experience, and of the largest study of these frontier questions, were strenuously, and are strenuously, and inflexibly, opposed to this war. (*Cheers.*) Let me add that just as strenuous opponents are found among Anglo-Indians. My right hon'ble friend knows that perfectly well. I am the last man to speak without respect and sympathy of the soldiers, the efforts and suffering of the soldiers in the field in this expedition, and all the heroic qualities which such scenes as these have brought forth. They are to some extent a partial compensation for all the wretchedness and destruction of the war. But we do not appreciate that any the less, because we think that the policy of these operations was a most erroneous and ill-conceived policy. (*Cheers.*) I am saying nothing against the military advisers in their own field, but I think it was my right hon'ble friend himself who said the soldier was like fire. He is a good servant, but a bad master. Let us suppose for a moment that there was an overwhelming weight, which there was not, of military opinion in favour of our securing passes beyond the frontier. Does that for one instant justify British statesmen on washing their hands of all responsibility? A more monstrous doctrine I really cannot imagine. I set up an entirely counter case to Mr. Chamberlain's case. Control by the central authority is not to be so minute or detailed as to fetter and cripple those who are the agents and representatives of this country in difficult conditions abroad. At the same time it is the House of Commons at Westminster, it is the Cabinet in Downing Street, that is ultimately responsible. No; I am wrong. It is you who are ultimately responsible. (*Cheers.*) It is you who are ultimately responsible, for it is you who create and constitute the House of Commons, and it is you who determine who are the men and what are the principles which are to guide the House of Commons in regulating those vast and momentous affairs. (*Cheers.*) Mr. Chamberlain says, "I hope you will excuse me if we"—that is, the present Government—"have not quite the same confidence in our own infallibility." Well, I welcome any disclaimer of infallibility from that quarter. (*Laughter.*) We took up our line of action, we formed our judgment, not because we thought ourselves infallible, but because we thought and think that the final question of the propriety of occupying passes or other territory beyond the present frontier depended upon considerations, of great variety and force, political and financial considerations, which a Cabinet of Civilians in much better able, from the wider range and combination of its knowledge and of the arguments present to the minds of the members of such a body, to weigh and to comprehend, than the most brilliant soldier in India. Mr. Chamberlain said the night before last he thought there would be no difference between us and them when the discussion takes place. Well, I shall be happy to find that that is so. We shall receive after we assemble papers, and at all events we shall understand from the Government what their proposal is. But our contention, I am sure, will be that any occupation, any manufacture of roads, will be a departure from the only sound principle upon which, in the minds of the best authorities, you can carry on your frontier administration. They will say it is only roads, but if you occupy a pass it will mean forts and putting troops into them. Common sense and experience tell us that you will have on your hands people on both sides. I hope the Government will not drag us along that road. How many troops will they lock up and how many tens of thousands of pounds will they fling away? How will they persuade the people of India—you are taking their money for many years to come to pay for all those things—how will you persuade them, it will do any good to them? And now I come to what is much to the front. I have only one sentence to say upon it. Who is to pay? Some weeks ago I said that I had been told that the expenditure would be something like £10,000,000. The Chancellor of the Exchequer at Bristol, following me, said, "Oh, that is an extravagant over-estimate. Not over two-and-a-half millions." But now, I understood that the other day he said that there would be no demand made upon us. Well, I confess I don't understand—he is a man who never says anything without good foundation for it, but I don't understand what he means by his present position. But this is the point that I will put to you without fear, and I will put it without fear to any audience in England or in Scotland. You here are exulting in the vast magnitude of British dominions, in the might of your fleets, in the incomparable strength of your finance, in surpluses measured by millions and millions; and then you come upon India, stricken by light and famine, plagues and earthquakes, and you throw upon them the burden of operations undertaken not because the people of this country ever thought it necessary, not because the Government, as a result of the independent operations of their own minds, thought it necessary, but because a handful of military experts choose to say that they regard that as a policy that ought to be pursued.

In a later passage in his speech Mr. Morley added:—

You have had several speeches made which you have read at breakfast or supper time in the last fortnight, and here are three things which are foreshadowed and opened up in these speeches from eminent and responsible ministers. First, there is the possibility of further military operations on the North-West frontier of India; second, isolated action, which Mr. Chamberlain foreshadows, in respect to Crete; third, war arising out of the position in China. You have those three contingencies. Heaven knows whether they will come. I trust they are remote, but responsible men raise them in discussion. We must face them, and recognise it as possible. They may happen or they may not, but ministers themselves tell you they have no more engagements than these three sets of demands upon your resources. I ask you as men of sense and sober judgment—agree with us about the domestic policy as you like—I ask whether with such contingencies before us, it is not preposterous to lock up a large number of British forces in the Soudan. I ask whether that deserves to be called by another name than preposterous.

APPENDIX D.

THE STUPENDOUS FABRIC OF GOVERNMENT IN INDIA.

[*Mr. John Morley, in the course of an address to his constituents at Bervie, in the Montrose Burghs, on June* 6, 1901, *said :—*]

I am only certain of one thing, and that is that amidst all these clouds that now overhang the horizon of British politics, the politician who despairs or loses his spirits or loses heart is a politician who puts himself out of Court. They call me a pessimist. I think that in one of these burghs I once ventured to define a pessimist as a man who declines to say it as a gloriously fine day when it is raining cats and dogs; and if I have not faith and hope and (may I go on and say ?) charity—if I had not faith and hope and charity, I should not be wearing myself out in making speeches either here or anywhere else, but I should leave the fallen world to its fate. (*Cheers*). I can never lose my confidence—although the confidence of a humble individual like myself is of little consequence—I can never lose my confidence in the destinies of this kingdom. But the times are a little difficult. There is an old Greek joke of a sober man who found himself in the company of ten men who were not sober, and the ten men unanimously agreed that the one man was drunk. (*Laughter.*) And when I read the articles about my couple of speeches in this constituency, I rub my eyes and I feel as bewildered as this one unfortunate man among the ten roysterers and revellers. (*Laughter.*) They write and talk as if people of my way of talking were bent upon painting the world drab; as if we were callous and cold hearted to all the great ideals of British power, British strength, and British glory. A more ridiculous caricature no mortal hand could paint—a caricature of men in whom the sense of British kinship is at least as lively as those whom, I think, Professor Seeley calls the bombastic school, who froth and fume about loyalty and patriotism and try to dazzle us with glittering platitudes about empire. One would think that they really doubted their loyalty and patriotism and greatness in the constantly talking of it. I do not talk of it, because I have other things to talk about. I take it for granted—and I hope you take it for granted—that I am just as proud of being a citizen of this enormous realm as any of those gentlemen. (*Cheers.*) I have said—I never will cease saying as long as it may, unfortunately, be required—I have said before we are all of one mind in seeking a strong and constant play between the Britons in the island home and Britons all over the globe who have carried loyalty to our institutions, our national freedom, and our strenuous industry to their homes over the sea. How could we who seek democratic ends, we who call ourselves Radicals—how could we fail to sympathise with and to admire our fellow-countrymen over the seas who find order and prosperity and growth and progress compatible with these—no State Church, payment of members, no House of Lords?—(*Cheers.*) How could we fail to sympathise with our fellow-countrymen across the seas who have solved these problems, for instance, which we have not yet quite solved? (*Cheers.*) The only difference between us in this, that those who are always taunting us with our want of Imperial instinct because we don't at once accept this or that nostrum of federal union, or I know not what; they don't distinguish, and I put my point of view to you in a homely expression. We believe that when you have two bodies moving along, wishing to move in harmony and in union you ought not to have a rigid iron bar, you ought to have a rope, a good stout rope, which may be slack or taunt as circumstances may demand, I wonder how, long the heavenly bodies would go along, would move in their orbits in the harmony that we behold, if they were fastened to one another by bolts of adamant. So we and our colonies, those great commonwealths, shall get along best if the tie between us is not a fixed and a rigid tie, dependent upon an artificial centralisation, but is a silken tie of affection and of mutual loyalty, of mutual good sense, and of mutual desire to keep constant and steadfast company with one another. (*Cheers.*) This is clear that the events of the last year and-a-half in which the colonists, our colonial fellow-countrymen, with great manliness and daring co-operation in our military enterprises—one thing is becoming every day clearer to those who observe pretty closely how things are working out, and that is that a whole group of new problems are arising which will require the greatest and most careful consideration on the part of statesmen both on the other side of these great waters and on our own side. I have no stint—how can any rational man have a stint to his admiration for the splendid, I would almost say stupendous, fabric of government that Great Britain upholds for instance, in India? Who can fail to admire the zeal, the energy, the intelligence, the skill, the persistence with which generation after generation of Englishmen and Scotsmen have built up and maintained that fabric? And I am glad to observe—may I say in passing?—that the present Governor-General of India, Lord Curzon, a man of great zeal and indefatigable industry—that he, so far as I can observe, is showing no sign of joining that forward and aggresive school, perhaps, I ought to say that forward and expansive school, which has wrought so considerable mischief in India before now. Then turn to another part of the world—turn to Egypt. We may wish, and some do wish, that we had never committed ourselves to the occupations of Egypt twenty years ago. We may wish that Lord Salisbury's attempt in 1887 to get us out of Egypt had not been baulked by the mistake of another Power. We may wish that Lord Salisbury's design of 1887 had succeeded, but that does not prevent us from doing full justice to one of the greatest feats of British administration that has ever been performed during the twenty years of Lord Cromer's administration in Egypt. I, for one, have never said that we can escape frontier troubles either in India or anywhere else. I use a figure of Lord Salisbury's—where you have savage races, barbarous races over your frontier, it is the surge of civilisation, he said, meeting the surge or barbarism. But I make his remarks that the very fact, the very circumstance of these inevitable frontier troubles is the very reason why we should sedulously be on our guard against incurring any responsibility or provoking any trouble on our borders when by patient and prudent management we might well avoid them. After all, it is not the magnitude of your dominion that constitutes British greatness. It is the sound and the true-hearted character of the people of this kingdom. What is miscalled Imperialism, what is misnamed imperialism, leaves out of sight altogether our moral power in Europe, and it claims—it has such language as predominance, it has such claims as ascendancy. That is not the way in which the name of Britain became great and her power strong. That precedence in Europe which Britain has so long enjoyed, and has enjoyed to the advantage and the good of the whole combined world, did not rest upon land robbers. (*Cheers.*) It has rested upon the conviction in the mind of Europe and of the world that on the whole our aims when we intervened were unselfish and were disinterested, animated by those principles of justice and freedom which make all the difference between a progressive civilisation and a civilisation which is not progressive but retrograde. (*Cheers.*)

APPENDIX E.

DESPATCH ON THE REFORM PROPOSALS.

[*The following is the full text of Lord Morley's Despatch* :—]

I have to acknowledge the important despatch of the 1st October, 1908, in which I had submitted for approval and decision a group of constitutional reforms framed by Your Excellency in Council, in pursuance of a policy initiated more than two years ago. Your proposals in their present shape are the outcome of a tentative project placed in August last year, in the hands of Local Governments in India with instructions to consult important bodies and individuals representative of various classes of the community before putting their own conclusions before the Government of India. Those instructions, as you are very evidently justified in assuring me, were carried out with great care and thoroughness. After examining, moreover, the enormous mass of material gathered together in a prolonged operation, I gladly recognise the admirable industry, patience, thought and candour with which that material has been sifted by your Government and worked out into practical proposals, liberal in their spirit and comprehensive in their scope. I have taken all the pains demanded by their importance to secure special consideration of them in Council. It is a sincere satisfaction to me to find myself able to accept the substantial part of Your Excellency's scheme, with such modifications as would naturally occur to different minds in handling problems of remarkable difficulty in themselves and reasonably open to a wide variety of solution.

THE IMPERIAL ADVISORY COUNCIL.

The original proposal of an Imperial Advisory Council was based on the interesting and attractive idea of associating ruling Chiefs and territorial magnates of British India in the guardianship of common and Imperial interests and as a means of promoting more intimate relations among component parts of the Indian Empire. The general opinion of those whose assent and co-operation would be indispensable has proved adverse, and Your Excellency in Council now considers that the project should for the present not be proceeded with.

You still favour an Imperial Council composed only of ruling Chiefs. Lord Lytton made an experiment in this direction, but it remained without successful result. Lord Curzon afterwards proposed to create a Council composed exclusively of Princes contributing Imperial Service Troops, and deliberating on that subject exclusively. The opinion is pronounced that this also is likely to be unfruitful and ineffectual in practice. Your Excellency's project is narrower than the first of these two and wider than the second. I confess that, while entirely appreciating and sympathising with your object, I judge the practical difficulties in the way of such a Council assembling under satisfactory conditions to be considerable—the expense, precedence, and housing, for instance, even if there were no others—yet if not definitely constituted with a view to assembly it could possess little or no reality. It would obviously be a mistake to push the project unless it commands clear assent and approval of those whose presence in the Council would be essential to its success, and the opinions expressed in the replies with which you have furnished me lead me to doubt whether that condition can be secured. But in case Your Excellency still favours this proposal, which is in itself attractive, I do not wish to express dissent at this stage, and if, after consultation with the leading Chiefs, you are able to devise a scheme that is at once acceptable to them and workable in practice, I am not inclined to place any obstacle in the way of a full and fair trial and in any event the doubt I have expressed must not be taken as discouraging consultation with individual Chiefs according to the existing practice, for nobody with any part to play in Indian Government can doubt the manifold advantages of still further developing not only amicable but confidential relations of this kind with the loyal rulers in Indian States, possessed as they are of such peculiar authority and experience.

PROVINCIAL ADVISORY COUNCILS.

Next I agree with Your Excellency in the judgment that the question of a Council of Notables for British India only should not be entertained. I am inclined, further more, for my own part, to doubt whether the creation of Provincial Advisory Councils is likely to prove an experiment of any marked actual value. The origin of the demand for bodies of that character, whatever the strength of such a demand amounts to, is undoubtedly the desire for greater facilities in the discussion of public measures. Your Excellency indicates what strikes me as pointing in a more hopeful direction in the proposition that this claim for increased facilities of discussion should be met "rather by extending the powers, of the existing Legislative Councils than by setting up large rival Councils which must to some extent conflict with them." Large or small, such rivalry would be almost certain to spiring up, and from the first the new species of Council would be suspected as designed to be a check upon the old. As in the case of ruling Chiefs or of notables in British India, so here, informal consultation with the leading men of a locality would have most or all of the advantages of an Advisory Council without the many obvious disadvantages of duplicating political machinery.

ENLARGEMENT OF LEGISLATIVE COUNCILS.

From these proposals I pass to what is, and what you declared to be, the pith and substance of the despatch under reply. "The enlargement of the Legislative Councils," you say, "and the extension of their functions to the discussion of administrative questions are the widest, most deep-reaching and most substantial features of the scheme which we now put forward." This perfectly correct description evoked and justified the close scrutiny to which these features have been subjected in my Council, and I am glad to believe that the result reveals few elements of material difference.

Your Government have now felt bound to deal first with the Imperial Legislative Council and from that work downwards to the Councils in the Provinces. I gather, however, from your despatch of the 21st March, 1907, that you would at that time have preferred, as Lord Lansdowne had done in 1892, to build up the higher fabric on the foundation of the Provincial Councils. In your circular letter of the 24th August, 1907, you observed that the most logical and convenient mode of dealing with the question would have been first to discuss and settle the composition, the electorates and the powers of the Provincial Legislative Councils, and then to build up on the basis of these materials a revised constitution for the Imperial Council. In the absence of proposals from the Local Governments and Administrations, you were precluded from adopting this course, and therefore, you set tentatively before them the line on which first the Legislative Council of the Governor-General and thereafter those of Governors and Lieutenant-Governors might be constituted.

In your present letter you have followed the same order, but with the full materials before me such as are now supplied by local opinions, it appears to be both more convenient and, as you said, more logical to begin with the Provincial Councils and afterwards to consider the constitution of the Legislative Council of the Governor-General.

PROVINCIAL LEGISLATIVE COUNCILS.

The first question that arises touches the principle of representation. This is fully discussed in paragraphs 18 to 20, 26 to 31, and 34 of your letter. Citing previous discussions of the subject and referring to the precedent of the measures taken to give effect to the Statute of 1892, you adhere to the opinion that in the circumstances of India, representation by classes and interest is the only practicable method of embodying the principle in the constitution of the Legislative Councils. (paragraphs A. D.) You justly observe that the principle to be borne in mind is that the election by the wishes of the people is the ultimate object to be secured, whatever may be the actual machinery adopted for giving effect to it. (paragraph 29.) You consider that for certain limited interests Corporations of Presidency towns, Universities, Chambers of Commerce, planting communities and the like limited electorates must exist as at present, and you foresee no serious obstacle in carrying out arrangements for that purpose. Difficulties come into view when you go beyond these limited electorates and have to deal with large and widespread interests or communities, such as the landholding and professional classes, or with important minorities, such as Mahomedans in most provinces in India, and Sikhs in the Punjab. You dwell upon the great variety of conditions in the various provinces of the Indian Empire and the impossibility of applying any uniform system throughout, and your conclusion generally appears to be that class electorates should be framed where this is practicable and likely to lead to good results, and in their failure or defect it will be necessary to have recourse to nomination.

With the general principles advanced by Your Excellency in this chapter of our discussion I am in entire accord. I agree that to some extent class representation must be maintained in the limited electorates to which you refer, and here, as you point out, no serious obstacle is to be anticipated. I agree also that the Legislative Council should reflect the leading elements of the population at large and that no system of representation would be satisfactory if it did not provide for the presence in the Councils of sufficient representatives of communities so important as are the Mahommedans and the landed classes. But, in examining your plans for obtaining their representation, I am struck with the difficulty of securing satisfactory electoral bodies under them and with the extent to which, as you expect, nomination will be demanded to supply the deficiencies of election. The same awakwardness and perplexity appear in obtaining satisfactory representation of the Indian commercial classes where, as is found generally throughout India with very few exceptions, they have not established Associations or Chambers to represent their interests.

The case of landholders is discussed in paragraphs 27 to 29 of your letter with immediate reference to the Imperial Legislative Council, and the situation is just the same. If separate representation is to be secured for local Councils you will "find it impossible to make any definite proposal which would admit of general application." (Para 27). You see difficulties in devising a constituency that should consist only of landholders deriving a certain income from land (Para 28), and you point out with much force the objections to election by voluntary Associations. In these observations I agree, and especially in your remark that the recognition of Associations as electoral agencies should be regarded as a provisional arrangement to be maintained only until some regular electorate can be formed.

The same difficulties as you observe in paragraph 30 encounter the proposal to have a special electorate for Mahomedans in some Provinces, as in Bombay the Mahomedans are so scattered that common organisation for electoral purposes is thought impracticable. In other Provinces it is proposed to found a scheme partly on a property qualification and partly on a literary attainment; in others again it is suggested that recourse might be had to voluntary associations. One difficulty in regard to Mahomedans is not mentioned in your letter for the provision in Province of a special electorate giving them a definite proportion of the seats on the Council might involve the refusal to them in that Province of a right to vote in the territorial electorates of which rural and Municipal Boards will afford the basis. If that were not done they would evidently have a double vote, and this would probably be resented by other classes of the population.

ELECTORAL COLLEGES.

Without rejecting the various expedients suggested by Your Excellency for adoption in order to secure the adequate representation of these important classes on the Councils, I suggest for your consideration that the object in view might be better secured, at any rate in the more advanced Provinces in India, by a modification of the system of a popular electorate found on the principle of electoral Colleges. The use of this method is not in itself novel. It already exists in the group of District Boards and of Municipalities, which in several Provinces return members to the Provincial Councils. The election is not committed to the Boards or Municipalities directly. These bodies choose electors, who then proceed to elect the representative of the group. I will briefly describe the scheme that at present commends itself to me, and in order to make the method of working clear I will assume hypothetical figures for a given Province. Let it be supposed that the total population of the Province is 24 millions, of whom 15 millions are Hindus and 5 millions Mahomedans, and the number of members to be elected 12. Then since the Hindus are to Mahomedans as three to one, nine Hindus should be elected to three Mahomedans. In order to obtain these members, divide the Province into three electoral areas, in each of which three Hindus and one Mahomedan are to be returned. Then each of these areas constitute an electoral College consisting of, let us say, a hundred members. In order to preserve the proportion between the two religions, 75 of those should be Hindus and 25 Mahomedans. This electoral College should be obtained by calling upon the various electorates, which might be (a) substantial landowners paying not less than a fixed amount of land-revenue, (b) the members of rural or sub-divisional Boards, (c) the members of District Boards, and (d) the members of Municipal Corporations, to return to it such candidates as they desired, a definite number being allotted to each electorate. Out of those offering themselves and obtaining votes, the 75 Hindus who obtained the majority of votes should be declared members of the College, and the 25 Mussalmans who obtained the majority should similarly be declared elected. If the Mussalmans returned did not provide 25 members for the electoral College, the deficiency would be made good by nomination. Having thus obtained an electoral College containing of 75 Hindus and 25 Mussalmans, that body would be called upon to elect three representatives for the Hindus and one for the Mahomedans. Each member of the College would have only one vote and could vote for only one candidate. In this way it is evident that it would be in the power of each section of the population to return a member in the proportion corresponding to its own proportion to the total population.

In the same way the desired proportion could be obtained of any representatives of any particular interest, as, for instance, of landowners. All that is necessary would be to constitute the electoral College in such a way that the number of electors representing the land-owning interest should bear to the total number the same proportion as the members of Council representing that interest to be elected bear to the total number to be elected.

In this manner minorities would be protected against exclusion by majorities and all large and important section of the population would have the opportunity of returning members in proportion to their ratio to the total population. Their choice could in that event be exercised in the best possible way, that, namely, of popular election, instead of requiring Government to supply deficiencies by the dubious method of nomination.

I do not wish definitely to prescribe such a scheme for adoption, whether locally or universally, but I commend it to your consideration. It appears to offer an expedient by which the objections against a system of nomination may be avoided and it would work through a choice freely exercised by the electorate at large instead of by artificial electorates specially constituted for the purpose. No doubt it removes the primary voter by more than one stage from the ultimate choice and it does not profess to be simple. I can only say that it is quite as simple as any scheme for representation of minorities can ever be, the system of a single vote, which is an essential part of it. It is said to work satisfactorily in places where it is in existence, and it is easy of apprehension by the electors. It would have several great advantages. It would bring the classes specially concerned within the popular electorate, and so meet the criticisms of the Hindus to which you refer in paragraph 30; second, it establishes a principle that would be an answer to further claims for representation by special classes or Associations; third, it would ensure the persons chosen being actually drawn from the locality that the electoral College represents; fourth, it would provide a healthy stimulus to interest in local self-government by linking up local bodies (Rural and Municipal Boards) more closely with the Provincial Legislative Councils. To this end it might be provided that the candidate for election to the Provincial Council must himself have taken part in local administration.

The due representation of the Indian mercantile community on which you touch in paragraph 31, of your letter, might be included in the scheme if the commercial classes fail to organise themselves as you suggest that they may arrange to do, in Associations similar to the European Chambers of Commerce.

To meet possible objections founded on the difficulty of bringing together electoral Colleges to vote in one place, I may add that this is not contemplated in the scheme. You refer at the close of paragraph 28 to the success of the Calcutta University in organising the election of Fellows by a large number of graduates scattered all over India. The votes of the electors in each College could, I imagine, be collected in the same manner without requiring them to assemble at a common centre.

OFFICIAL MAJORITY TO BE DISPENSED WITH.

From the electoral structure I now turn to the official element in the constitution of Provincial Legislative Councils dealt with in paragraphs 43 to 56 of your letter. I first observe that in all of them you provide for a bare official majority, but you contemplate that in ordinary circumstances only the number of official members necessary for the transaction of business shall be able to attend. The first question, therefore, is the necessity of maintaining in these Councils the majority of officials.

We have before us to begin with the leading fact that in the important Province of Bombay there is in the Council, as at present composed, no official majority, and that the Bombay Government, even in the smaller of its alternative schemes, presented to Your Excellency in Council is willing to dispense with such a majority, considering the character of the Legislation ordinarily coming before a Provincial Council. It is not possible with due representation given to the various classes and interests in the community to do without a majority of officials. After a careful consideration, I have come to the conclusion that in Provincial councils such a majority may be dispensed with provided that a substantial official majority is permanently maintained in the Imperial Legislative Council.

I do not conceal from myself the risks in such an arrangement. The non-official majority may press legislation of a character disapproved by the Executive Government. This should be met by the exercise of the power to withhold assent possessed by the head of the Government then. Although the local Legislature is vested with power to make laws for the peace and good government of the territories constituting the Province, still the range of subjects is considerably narrowed by the statutory exclusions now in force. Thus, for example, the local Legislature may not, without the previous sanction of the Governor-General make or take into consideration any law affecting the public debt of India or the Customs duties or any other tax or duty for the time being in force and imposed by the authority of the Governor-General in Council for the general purposes of the Government of India, or regulating currency or postal or telegraph business, or altering in any way the Indian Penal Code, or affecting religion or religious rites or usages, or affecting the discipline or maintenance of Naval or Military forces, or dealing with patents or copyright, or the relations of the Government with foreign Princes or States. It is difficult to see how any measure of such urgency that delay might work serious mischief can come before a Provincial Council; for mere opposition to a useful and beneficial project would not come within this description. On the other hand, and perhaps more often, there may be opposition on the part of the non-official Members to legislation that the Goverument desires. With a Council, however, representing divergent interests and realising together with its increased powers greater responsibility, a combination of all the non-official Members to resist a measure proposed by the Government would be unlikely, and some non-officials at least would probably cast their votes on the side of the Government. If, however, a combination of all the non-official members against the Government were to occur, that might be a very good reason for thinking that the proposed measure was really open to objection, and should not be proceeded with.

Your Excellency will recall since you came into the authority of Governor-General an Act proposed by a Local Government which a representative Legislative Council would almost certainly have rejected. Your Excellency's action in withholding assent from the Act shows that in your judgment it would have been an advantage if the Local Government had been induced by a hostile vote to reconsider their Bill. If, in spite of such hostile vote, the comparatively rare case should arise where immediate legislation were still thought absolutely necessary, then the constitution as at present stands provides an adequate remedy. The Governor-General in Council to-day possesses a concurrent power to legislate for any Province, and though I strongly favour a policy that would leave to each local Legislature the duty of providing for its own requirements, still I recognise in this power an ample safeguard, should, under exceptional circumstances, a real demand for its exercise arise.

CONSTITUTION OF PROVINCIAL COUNCILS.

This decision will make it necessary to modify to some extent the constitution of the several Provincial Councils proposed by you and will enable you to secure a wider representation. Subject to consideration of these details (which will not involve the postponement of the proposed Parliamentary Legislation for the amendment of the Indian Councils Act, 1892, and for other purposes), I am ready to accept generally the proposals for numbers and the constitution of the Councils set forth in your letter.

THE IMPERIAL LEGISLATIVE COUNCIL.

Your proposals in relation to the Imperial Legislative Council are necessarily entitled to the greatest weight. I am glad to find msyelf able to accept them practically in their entirety. While I desire to liberalise as far as possible the Provincial Councils, I recognise that it is an essential condition of this policy that the Imperial supremacy shall be in no degree compromised. I must, therefore, regard it as essential that Your Excellency's Council in its legislative as well as its executive character should continue to be so constituted as to ensure its constant and uninterrupted power to fulfil the constitutional obligations that it owes and must always owe to His Majesty's Government and to the Imperial Parliament. I see formidable drawbacks that have certainly not escaped Your Excellency to the expedient which you purpose, and I cannot regard with favour the power of calling into play an official majority while seeming to dispense with it. I am unable to persuade myself that to import a number of gentlemen to vote down something upon which they may or may not have heard the arguments will prove satisfactory. To secure the required relations, I am convinced that a permanent official majority in the Imperial Legislative Council is absolutely necessary, and this must outweigh the grave disadvantages that induce us to dispense with it in the Provincial Legislatures. It need not be in any sense an overwhelming majority, and this Your Excellency does not seek, but it must be substantial as it is certainly desirable that the Governor-General should be removed from the conflict of the division list and that the fate of any measure or Resolution should not rest on his vote alone.

I have already dealt in the earlier paragraphs of this Despatch with the elective principle, and it will be for Your Excellency to consider how far the popular electorate can be utilised for the return to your Legislative Council of landholders and Mahomedans. Some modifications of the scheme suggested for the Provinces will, no doubt, be necessary, and the electoral Colleges would probably have to be on the basis of Province and not of division, and the case of the Central Provinces would probably (in view of the disappearance of Advisory Councils) have to be met by nomination until a local Legislature is provided.

I accept your proposals for securing the representation of commerce both European and Indian.

I also agree to your proposals as to nomination, but it will be a matter for your consideration whether to meet the requirement of a substantial official majority. The number of nominated officials should not be raised.

Your plan for securing occasional representation for the interest of minorities such as the Sikhs, the Parsis, the Indian Christians, the Buddhists and the domiciled community meets with my entire approval, and I am in complete sympathy with your intention sometimes to appoint one or two experts in connection with legislation pending before Council.

INCREASED FACILITIES FOR DEBATE.

I turn to the proposals contained in paragraph 57-59 of your despatch affording further facilities for debate. This subject, as your Excellency remarks, was not dealt with in the earlier correspondence out of which your present proposals arise, but I am entirely in accord with your Excellency's Government in regarding it as of cardinal importance.

The existing law which confines discussion, except on the occasion of the Annual Financial Statement, to the Legislative proposals actually before the Council imposes a restriction that I am convinced is no longer either desirable or necessary. The plan of Your Excellency's Government contemplates a wide relaxation of this restriction, and in sanctioning it generally I am confident that these increased facilities, judiciously used, will be pronounced of the greatest advantage, not only by Councils and those whom they represent but also by Government who will gain additional opportunities both of becoming acquainted with the drift of public opinion and of explaining their own actions.

EFFECT OF THE RESOLUTIONS.

Taking the proposals in detail, I agree that the Resolutions to be moved should take the form of recommendations to Government, having only such force and effect as Government after consideration shall deem due to them. The introduction and discussion of Resolutions should not extend to subjects removed from the cognisance of Legislative Councils by Statute, and must obviously be subject to rules and restrictions. These, as Your Excellency observes, may best be laid down in the first place when the rules of business are drawn up and developed thereafter as experience may show to be desirable. Meanwhile, I agree generally with the conditions suggested in paragraph 59 of your despatch. I must, however, remark upon the first of the suggested conditions that isolated incidents of administration or personal questions may be and often are at the same time matters of public and general importance. It would, in my opinion, be sufficient to lay down that Resolutions must relate to matters of public and general importance, inasmuch as the President of the Council will have the power of deciding finally whether any proposed Resolution does, or does not, satisfy this condition.

INTERPELLATION.

In respect of rules on the asking of questions I have come to the conclusion that subject to such restrictions as may be found requisite in practice and to the existing general powers of the President, the asking of supplementary questions should be allowed. Without these a system of formal questions met by formal replies must inevitably tend to become unreal and ineffective and in an assembly in which, under proper safeguards, free discussion and debate is permitted and encouraged, there can be no sufficient reason for prohibiting that method of eliciting information and expressing indirectly the opinions and wishes of the questioners.

DISCUSSION OF THE IMPERIAL BUDGET.

Special importance attaches to rules as to the discussion of the Imperial Budget and I recognise with much satisfaction the liberality of the proposals that you have placed before me. The changes under this head constitute a notable step in the direction of giving to the representatives of Indian opinion a part in the most important administrative operation of the political year. I approve the dates suggested for the promulgation of the Financial Statement and for the beginning and ending of its discussion in Committee, and I anticipate valuable results from the knowledge which your Government will acquire in these debates of the views of those whom the proposed measures will chiefly and directly affect, and which it will be able to utilise in shaping its final financial proposals for the year. Generally, also, I approve the rules sketched in paragraph 64 for the regulation of discussions in Committee and of the moving of Resolutions and I concur in your opinion that the form of procedure should be such as to show clearly that the power of executive action resides exclusively in Government, who, while inviting the free expression of opinion in the form of Resolutions, do not thereby forego any part of the power and responsibility which has been and must continue to be in their hands.

PROVINCIAL BUDGETS.

Your proposals for the discussion of the Provincial Budgets seem entirely sound. As in the case of the Imperial Budget, so with respect to the Provincial finances, I observe with satisfaction that provision is made for full and free discussion and for the consideration by Government of the results of such discussion before the final proposals for the year are framed, and I believe that under the system suggested by you the Local Governments will retain that ultimate control over the financial policy of their Provinces, without which not only the authority of the Government of India but also that of the Secretary of State in Council and of Parliament would inevitably disappear.

FURTHER REFORMS.

Your Excellency claims for your scheme as a whole "that it will really and effectively" associate the people of India in the work not "only of occasional legislation but of actual every-day administration." The claim is abundantly justified, yet the scheme is not and hardly pretends to be a complete representation of the entire body of changes and improvements in the existing system that are evidently present to the minds of some of those whom your Government has consulted and that to the best of my judgment are now demanded by the situation described in the opening words of the despatch. It is evidently desirable, Your Excellency will agree, to present our reformed constitutional system as a whole. From this point of view it seems necessary to attempt without delay in effectual advance in the direction of local self-government.

LOCAL SELF-GOVERNMENT.

The principles that should inspire and regulate measures with this aim can hardly be laid down in sounder or clearer terms than in the Resolution published by the Government of India on the 18th May, 1882. I do not know where to look for a better expression of the view that should govern our policy under this important head, and I will venture to quote some passages in this memorable deliverance. Explaining the proposal for local self-government of that date the Government of India place themselves on ground which will be our ground also. "It is not primarily," they say, "with a view to improvement in administration that the measure is put forward and supported, it is chiefly desirable as an instrument of political and popular education," and again "there appears to be great force in the argument that so long as the chief Executive officers are, as a matter of course, Chairmen of the Municipal and District Committees there is little chance of these Committees affording any effective training to their members in the management of local affairs or of the non-official members taking any real interest in local business. The non-official members must be led to feel that real power is placed in their hands and that they have real responsibilities to discharge." This anticipation has been, to some extent, warranted by experience. Funds have not existed for an efficient Executive staff. The official element within the local bodies has been in many places predominant. Non-official members have not been induced to such an extent as was hoped to take a real interest in local business because their powers and their responsibilities were not real. If Local Self-Government has so far been no marked success as a training ground, it is mainly for the reason that the constitution of the local bodies departed from what was affirmed in the Resolution to be "the true principle" that "the control should be exercised from without rather than from within; the Government should revise and check the acts of local bodies but not dictate them." I have no doubt that the Government of India to-day will affirm and actively shape their policy upon the principle authoritatively set forth by their predecessors in 1882:—"It would be hopeless to expect any real development of self-government if the local bodies were subject to check and interference in matters of details, and the respective powers of Government and of various local bodies should be clearly and distinctly defined by statute, so that there may be as little risk of friction and misunderstanding as possible within the limits to be laid down in each case. However the Governor-General in Council is anxious that the fullest possible liberty of action should be given to local bodies."

THE STARTING POINT IN PUBLIC LIFE.

Your Excellency will recall that the Resolution from which I have quoted treats the sub-division, taluka or the tahsil as the smallest administrative unit. It is a question whether it would not be a wise policy to go further. The village in India (generally) has been the fundamental and indestructible unit of the social system, surviving the downfall of dynasty after dynasty. I desire Your Excellency in Council to consider the best way of carrying out a policy that would make the village a starting point of public life.

A SPECIAL DEPARTMENT.

The encouragement of local self-government being an object of such high importance in the better organisation of our Indian system, it remains to be considered how far in each Province it would be desirable to create a department for dealing exclusively with these local bodies, guiding and instructing them and correcting abuses in a form analogous to the operations of the Local-Government Board in this country. That, however, is a detail, though a weighty one in a question on which as a whole I confidently expect that Your Excellency will find much light in the forthcoming report of the Royal Commission on Decentralisation.

EXECUTIVE COUNCILS: ADMISSIONS OF INDIANS.

In the closing page of your letter Your Excellency raises a question of a high order of importance. You recognise as you inform me that the effect of our proposals will be to throw a greater burden on the heads of Local Governments, not only by reason of that actual increase of work caused by the long sittings of the Legislative Councils, but also because there will be considerable responsibility in dealing with the recommendations of those Councils. You then suggest the possibility that experience may show it to be desirable to strengthen the hands of the Lieutenant-Governors in the large Provinces by the creation of Executive Councils and of assisting the Governors of Madras and Bombay by enlarging the Executive Councils that now exist in these Presidencies.

I have to observe with respect to Bombay and Madras that the original scheme under the Act of 1833 provided for the appointment of three Members in these Presidencies. It seems conformable to the policy of this Despatch to take the power to raise to four the numbers of each of these Executive Councils of whom one, at least, should be an Indian. I would not, however, propose to make this a provision of a statute but would leave it to practice and usage growing into confirmed rule.

MORE EXECUTIVE COUNCILS IN THE LARGER PROVINCES.

As to the creation of Executive Councils in the larger Provinces, I am much impressed by both of the considerations that weigh with Your Excellency in throwing out the suggestion and more especially by the second of them. All will depend for the wise and efficient despatch of public business upon right relations between the supreme head of the Executive power in the Province and the Legislative Council. The question is whether these relations will be the more likely to adjust themselves effectively if the judgment of the Lieutenant-Governor is fortified and enlarged by two or more competent advisers with an official and responsible share in his deliberations.

Your Excellency anticipates longer sittings of the Legislative Council with increased activity of discussion, and the effectual representation of Provincial opinion and feeling as a guide to executive authority is the central object of the policy of Your Excellency's despatch. The aim of that policy is twofold, at once to enable Government the better to realise the wants, interests and sentiment of the governed, and on the other hand to give the governed a better chance of understanding, as occasion arises, the case for Government against the misrepresentations of ignorance and malice. The double object, as Your Excellency fully appreciates, is the foundation of the whole system in India and all over the world of administration and legislation either through or subject to the criticism of deliberative bodies, whether great or small.

The suggestion for the establishment of the Executive Councils for Lieutenant-Governors, as Your Excellency is aware, is not new. A really new problem of new solution is in truth surprisingly uncommon in the history of British rule in India and of the political or administrative controversies connected with it. Indeed, without for an instant undervaluing the supreme necessity for caution and circumspection at every step and motion in Indian Government, it may be open to some question whether in some of these controversies before now even an erroneous conclusion would not have been better than no conclusion at all. The issue we are now considering was much discussed in obedience to the orders of the Secretary of State in 1868 by men of the highest authority on Indian questions and I do not conceive that after all the consideration given to the subject then and since, further consultations could be expected to bring any new arguments of weight and substance into view.

It has sometimes been argued that the creation of Executive Councils in the major Provinces would necessarily carry with it as in Bombay and Madras the appointment in each case of a Governor from Home. This would indeed be a "large departure from the present system of administration, almost amounting to the confusion and overthrow of that system reposing as it does upon the presence at the head of the highest administrative posts of officers trained and experienced in the complex requirements and diversified duties of the Indian Government. I take for granted, therefore, that the head of the Province will be, as now, a member of the Indian Civil Service appointed in such mode as the law prescribes.

THE POWER OF VETO.

I propose, therefore, to ask for power to create Executive Councils from time to time as may be found expedient. In this connection, we cannot ignore the necessity of securing that a constitutional change designed both to strengthen the authority and to lighten the labours of the head of the Province shall not impair the prompt exercise of Executive power. It will, therefore, be necessary to consider most carefully what degree of authority over the members of his Council in case of dissent should be vested in the head of a Province in which an Executive Council may be called into being. It was recognised by Parliament more than a century ago that the Governors of Madras and Bombay should be vested with a discretionary power of overruling these Councils in cases of high importance and essentially affecting the public interest and welfare. A power no less than this will obviously be required in the Provinces in which a Council may come to be associated with the head of the Executive, and I shall be glad if you will favour me with your views upon its definition. Your Excellency will readily understand that the use of such a power, while not to be evaded in the special cases for which it is designed, is not intended for a part of the ordinary mechanism of Government. Rather, in the language of the historical despatch of 1834, it is my belief that "in a punctual, constant and ever fastidious adherence to your ordinary rules of practice you will find the best security not only for the efficiency and also for the despatch of your Legislative proceedings."

APPENDIX F.

KING EDWARD'S MESSAGE.

[*The following is the message to the Princes and peoples of India issued on the occasion of the fiftieth year of the transfer of Indian administration from the East India Company to the British throne. This message published on Nov. 2, 1908 is well-known as the handiwork of Lord Morley.*]:—

It is now 50 years since Queen Victoria, My beloved Mother, and My August Predecessor on the Throne of these Realms, for divers weighty reasons, with the Advice and Consent of Parliament, took upon herself the Government of the territories theretofore administered by the East India Company. I deem this a fitting anniversary on which to greet the Princes and Peoples of India, in commemoration of the exalted task then solemnly undertaken. Half a century is but a brief span in your long annals, yet this half a century that ends to-day will stand amid the floods of your historic ages, a far-shining landmark. The Proclamation of the direct supremacy of the Crown sealed the unity of Indian Government and opened a new era. The journey was arduous, and the advance may have sometimes seemed slow; but the incorporation of many strangely diversified communities, and of some three hundred millions of the human race, under British guidance and control has proceeded steadfastly and without pause. We survey Our labours of the past half a century with clear gaze and good conscience.

Difficulties such as attend all human rule in every age and place, have risen up from day to-day. They have been faced by the servants of the British Crown with toil and courage and patience, with deep counsel and a resolution that has never faltered nor shaken. If errors have occurred, the agents of My Government have spared no pains and no self-sacrifice to correct them; if abuses have been proved, vigorous hands have laboured to apply a remedy.

No secret of empire can avert the scourge of drought and plague, but experienced administrators have done all that skill and devotion are capable of doing to mitigate those dire calamities of Nature. For a longer period than was ever known in your land before, you have escaped the dire calamities of War within your borders. Internal peace has been unbroken.

In the great Charter of 1858 Queen Victoria gave you noble assurance of Her earnest desire to stimulate the peaceful industry of India, to promote works of public utility and improvement, and to administer the Government for the benefit of all resident therein. The schemes that have been diligently framed and executed for promoting your material convenience and advance—schemes unsurpassed in their magnitude and their boldness—bear witness before the world to the zeal with which that benignant promise has been fulfilled.

The rights and privileges of the Feudatory Princes and Ruling Chiefs have been respected, preserved, and guarded; and the loyalty of their allegiance has been unswerving. No man among My subjects has been favoured, molested, or disquieted, by reason of his religious belief or worship. All men have enjoyed protection of the law. The law itself has been administered without disrespect to creed or caste or to usages and ideas rooted in your civilisation; it has been simplified in form, and its machinery adjusted to the requirements of ancient communities slowly entering a new world.

The charge confided to My Government concerns the destinies of countless multitudes of men now and for ages to come, and it is a paramount duty to repress with a stern arm guilty conspiracies that have no just cause and no serious aim. These conspiracies I know to be abhorrent to the loyal and faithful character of the vast hosts of My Indian subjects, and I will not suffer them to turn Me aside from my task of building up the fabric of security and order.

Unwilling that this historic anniversary should pass without some signal mark of Royal Clemency and Grace, I have directed that, as was ordered on the memorable occasion of the Coronation Durbar in 1903, the sentences of persons whom Our Courts have duly punished for offences against the law, should be remitted, or in various degrees reduced; and it is My wish that such wrong-doers may remain mindful of this act of Mercy, and may conduct themselves without offence henceforth.

Steps are being continuously taken towards obliterating distinctions of race as the test for access to posts of public authority and power. In this path I confidently expect and intend the progress henceforward to be steadfast and sure, as education spreads, experience ripens and the lessons of responsibility are well learned by the keen intelligence and apt capabilities of India.

From the first, the principle of representative institutions began to be gradually introduced, and the time has come when, in the judgment of My Viceroy and Governor-General and others of My Counsellors, that principle may be prudently extended. Important classes among you, representing ideas that have been fostered and encouraged by British rule, claim equality of citizenship, and a greater share in legislation and Government. The politic satisfaction of such a claim will strengthen, not impair, existing authority and power. Administration will be all the more efficient, if the officers who conduct it have greater opportunities of regular contact with those whom it affects, and with those who influence and reflect common opinion about it. I will not speak of the measures that are now being diligently framed for these objects. They will speedily be made known to you, and will, I am very confident, mark a notable stage in the beneficent progress of your affairs.

I recognise the valour and fidelity of My Indian troops, and at the new year I have ordered that opportunity should be taken to show in substantial form this, My high appreciation, of their martial instincts, their splendid discipline, and their faithful readiness of service.

The welfare of India was one of the objects dearest to the heart of Queen Victoria. By Me, ever since My visit in 1875, the interests of India, its Princes and peoples, have been watched with an affectionate solicitude that time cannot weaken. My dear Son, the Prince of Wales, and the Princess of Wales, returned from their sojourn among you with warm attachment to your land, and true and earnest interest in its well-being and content. These sincere feelings of active sympathy and hope for India on the part of My Royal House and Line, only represent, and they do most truly represent, the deep and united will and purpose of the people of this Kingdom.

May Divine protection and favour strengthen the wisdom and mutual good will that are needed for the achievement of a task as glorious as was ever committed to Rulers and Subjects in any State or Empire of recorded time.

APPENDIX G.

THE INDIAN VICEROYALTY.

[*In the course of his article on "British Democracy and Indian Government" in the Nineteenth Century and After, for February 1911, Lord Morley discusses at length the relation of the Viceroy and the Secretary of State for India and we extract that portion below*] :—

In view of the great general question how the omnipotence of democracy and all its influences, direct and indirect are likely to affect Indian rule, the particular question of the relations between the Secretary of State and the Governor-General in Council is cardinal. It is not a branch of the main issue, it is in fact, a trunk. Mr. Chirol looks to the greatest possible decentralisation in India subject to the general, but unmeddlesome, control of the Governor-General in Council, and to the greatest possible freedom of the Government of India from all interference from home, except in regard to those broad principles of policy which it must always rest with the Imperial Government, represented by the Secretary of State in Council, to determine. This is well enough, but Mr. Chirol knows far too much of the range of administration not to beware this his exposition is too loose to be a real guide in every day practice. The difficulty arises in the demands of each particular case. A Local Government for instance, proposes a stiff campaign of prosecution for sedition. The Viceroy in Council, on the broader grounds of his policy at the time, disapproves. Who is to decide whether his disapproval and disallowance are unmeddlesome? In this diametrical opposition of view, is the Lieutenant-Governor or the Governor-General in Council to have the last and decisive word? So in larger issues. A Viceroy insists that a particular change in Military administration is unwise, and at any rate the appointment of a certain Military Officer would be the best if the change were accepted. How can we say on broad principles of policy whether the Cabinet would be justified in overruling the Viceroy on either limb of the business, until we have investigated all the circumstances of qualification and personality. And is it not upon this investigation that the applicability of the broad principle, whatever it may be, and if you were quite sure of being lucky enough to find it, must necessarily depend? It would be easy to find a hundred illustrations, some known to all the world, many more of them judiciously hidden away to dusty eternity in pigeon holes and tin boxes. Suppose a parliamentary debate were to arise. For one argument turning on a broad principle, a score, and those the most effective, would turn upon items of circumstances.

There has been, in both Indian and English journals, much loose, inaccurate, and ill-informed argument on this important matter during the last six or seven years. This is what makes it well worth while to clear up some of the confusion, certainly not for the dubious pleasure of fighting old battles over again, but to reach a firm perception of the actual constitution of Indian Government with a view to future contingencies that might at any time arrest the attention of Cabinets or Parliaments. The controversy came into full blaze in 1905, when as Mr. Chirol puts it, (p. 34), the Viceroy of the day felt himself compelled to resign because he was overruled by the Home Government. Mr. Chirol seems to accept, though not without something like reluctance, the only tenable principle, namely, that the ultimate responsibility for Indian Government rests unquestionably with the imperial Government represented by the Secretary of State for India and therefore in the last resort with the people of the United Kingdom represented by Parliament. This is incontestable as will be shown in a few moments and no responsible person in either of the two Houses will ever dream of getting up to contest it even in days when such singular anxiety prevails to find new doctrines and devices for giving the House of Commons the slip. Nobody will dispute that the Cabinet are just as much masters over the Governor-General as they are over any other servant of the Crown. The Cabinet, through a Secretary of State, have an inexpugnable right, subject to law, to dictate policy, to mitigate instructions, to reject proposals, to have the last word on every question that arises and the first word in every question that in their view ought to arise. On no other terms could our Indian system come within the sphere of Parliamentary Government. Withour trying to define political relations in language of legal precision we cannot shut our eyes to the obvious fact that where the Secretary of State or the Prime Minister has to answer a challenge in Parliament on Indian business he could not shield himself behind the authority of the Governor-General nor could he plead, except in expenditure, the opinion or action of the Indian Council at Whitehall.

What does Mr. Chirol say? The doctrine of the Governor-General in Council being the agent—as he has been called—of the Cabinet, 'ignores one of the most important features of his office—one indeed to which supreme importance attaches in a country such as India, where the sentiment of reverence for the sovereign is rooted in the most ancient traditions of all races and creeds.' 'The Viceroy,' Mr. Chirol proceeds, 'is the direct and personal representative of the King-Emperor, and in that capacity, at any rate, it would certainly be improper to describe him as the agent of the Secretary of State.' In all that follows as to the importance of upholding the figure of the Governor-General, nobody concurs more whole-heartedly than the present writer. As Lord Salisbury once said, 'I hold the monarchy must seem to be as little constitutional as possible. Still, any serious politician, with the sincerest respect for all the solemn plausibilities of these stately, imposing and substantially important human things will be incorrigibly slow to believe that either this great officer or any other servant of the Crown is, or can be, constitutionally withdrawn from Ministerial control. Nor is it easy to discover any good foundation either in law or established practice for the contrary doctrine. Mr. Disraeli writing to Queen Victoria about the new law of 1858, spoke of further steps that were necessary to influence the opinion and affect the imagination of the Indian populations. "The name of Your Majesty ought to be impressed on their native life." Nor will any wise man deny the enormous political value in India of all the ideas that are associated with the thought of personal sovereignty. This is a different question, or, in fact, it is no question at all. But let us distinguish. In the debates of 1858, the direct connection with the Crown was recognised as of great importance by Lord Palmerston and others but among the resolutions on which the Bill was founded, was this as finally reported: That, for this purpose *i.e.*, transfer of the Crown] it is expedient to provide that Her Majesty, by one of the responsible Ministers of the Crown, shall have and perform all the powers and duties relating to the Government and Revenues of India......which are or may be now exercised and performed by the old Board of Control and Directors of the East India Company. There is nothing here about direct personal representation; the unmistakable implication is exactly the opposite. What is or is not constitutional quality in act or policy, as innumerable debates are now showing, takes on to slippery ground. Happily for our immediate purpose, the Indian system is a written one, resting on statute and instruments as good as statute. Mr. Chirol, as I have said, admits that responsibility rests unquestionably with the Home Government represented by the Indian Secretary. Yet, he has tried his hand at making out a case for limitation of the Indian Secretary's power, authority and duties, so severe as to make authority perilously shadowy and second-hand. His examination of the texts bearing on the matter hardly profess to be exhaustive and its implications must be pronounced somewhat misleading. Let us see. In 1858, Queen Victoria announced to the Princes, Chiefs and Peoples of India that she had taken upon herself the government of the territories in India heretofore administered in trust for her by the East India Company and further: "We reposing especial trust and confidence in the loyalty, ability and judgment of our right, trusty and well-beloved cousin......constitute and appoint him to be our first Viceroy and Governor-General in and over said territories and to administer the Government thereof in our name and on our behalf, subject to such rules and regulations as he shall from time to time receive through one of our Principal Secretaries of State. The principle so definitely announced has been uniformly maintained. The Royal Warrant appointing the Governor-General always contains the provision thus set forth in the Mutiny Proclamation. 'Now, know that we reposing especial limit and confidence in the Fidelity, Prudence, Justice and Circumspection of you the said Victor Alexander, Earl of Elgin and Kincardine, have nominated and appointed you to be Governor-General of India......to take upon you, hold and enjoy the said office during our Will and Pleasure subject nevertheless to such instructions and directions as you...shall as Governor-General of India in Council from time to time receive under the hand of one of our Principal Secretaries of State.' This language of the Mutiny Proclamation and of the Warrants of Appointment clench the question so far as the Governor-General in Council is concerned.

The position, on the other hand, of the Secretary of State under the statutes is quite as clear though it takes a few more words to set it out and a trifle more trouble to follow. The law of 1858, calling the Indian Secretary into existence, enacts that 'same as herein otherwise provided one of Her Majesty's Principal Secretary of State shall have and perform all such or the like powers and duties in anywise relating to the Government of Revenues of India and all such of the like powers over all officers appointed or continued under this Act as might or should have been exercised or performed by the East India Company or by the Court of Directors or Court of Proprietors of the said Company." This section continues to the Secretary of State all the powers of the Company and the relations of the Company to their Governor-General were defined in the Regulating Act of 1772. 'The said Governor-General and Council for the time being shall, and they are hereby directed and required to obey all such orders as they shall receive from the Court of Directors of the said United Company.' Then by the Act of 1784, which plays so famous a party both in his own career and in party and political history, Pitt called into existence the body of Commissioners who became known as the Board of Control. Their business, as set forth eight years later, was 'to have and be invested with full power and authority to superintend, direct and control all acts, operations, and concerns which in anywise relate to or concern the Civil or Military Government or revenues of the said territories and acquisition in the East Indies.' All these powers and duties, formerly vested either in the Board of Control or in the Company, the Directors and the Secret Committee in respect of the Government and revenues of India were to be inherited by the Indian Secretary. In short, as it is plainly summed up in that magnificient enterprise, the 'Imperial Gazetteer of India' composed, I think, officially at Simla, the Secretary of state 'has the power of giving orders to every officer in India, including the Governor-General.' It may seem waste of time to labour all this, as if we were foreign to what twenty years ago at any rate was a wide open door. Though occasional phrases of a splenetic turn may be found in the printed correspondence of Governor-General, there has never been any serious pretension to deny, dispute or impair the patent truth that the Cabinet is the single seat of final authority. One powerful Viceroy, in a famous speech full of life and matter did indeed declare that if the day should ever come when the Governor-General of India is treated as the mere puppet or mouthpiece of the Home Government required only to carry out whatever orders it may be thought desirable to transmit, then the post should cease to exist. To be sure it should; everybody would agree, just as they would at least profess to agree in rejecting the still more absurd counter-doctrine, that the Home Government should be the puppet of an infallible Man on the Spot. The clash should never arise, and, in fact, very rarely has arisen. The only security that can be found for the smooth working, of what is undeniably an extremely delicate piece of machinery must be sought in the right judgment of the two parties; in their common feeling of responsibility, in patience, mutual regard, concord in fundamentals if not in every circumstantial—and perhaps with no personal leaning to astrology—I may add the contribution, named by Machiavelli in his famous chapter on the part played in human things by Fortune and the Stars, with common sense and good luck—not the most modest of demands—all goes well. Nowhere in the whole huge and diversified structure of what is called the Empire, do the personal elements and their right balance of equanimity and energy count for more than they count in India.

APPENDIX H.

INDIAN UNREST

[*Lord Morley, reviewing Mr. Chirol's book in the "Nineteenth Century and After'*,' *for February 1911, makes the following observations on "The Unrest in India"*]:—

All depends upon the common recognition among those who have the power of moulding public opinion and whom the public listen to, that elementary truth of political principles if not ethical standards are relative to times, reasons, social climate and tradition. Everybody now realises this in judging old history. It is the beginning and end of wisdom in the new history that Parliament has its share in helping to make Asia to-day. To insist on applying rationalistic general ideas to vast communities, living on mysticism, can do no good to either governors or governed. It is hard for rationalism and mysticism to be friends and their interplay is no easy game. Overweening pretensions as to the superiority, at every point and in all their aspects, of any Western civilisation over every Eastern is fundamental error. If we pierce below the varnish of words, we anyhow uncover state of barbarism in the supreme capitals and centres, whether in Europe or in the two great continents of North and South America. The Indian student in London, Edinburgh and New York finds this out and reports it.

Even those who do not wholly share Christ's interpretation of the array of facts he has marshalled, will recognise a serious attempt by a competent hand to induce the public to get within the minds of the millions whose political destinies they have taken into their hands. Gœthe, when at a certain stage in culture he turned his thoughts Eastward. found China barren, and India 'a jumble.' It is little wonder if the ordinary Englishman feels as Gœthe felt. The scene is distant, names are not easy to distinguish or appreciate, terms are technical, or the heart that pulses under the brown skin seems impenetrable, a mysterious veil hangs over the stage actors and drama. Then our democracy is very busy, and its betters have pursuits that pass for business.

Of the three great historic faiths, Christianity, Buddhism, Islam, Hinduism has resisted two, and in only a small degree accepted one. By Western it is the least easy of the three to grasp, yet even the general reader would find himself instructed, interested and fascinated in such writings as the second series of Sir Alfred Lyall's Asiatic Studies, Max Muller's Cambridge Lectures, and some chapters especially VII, VIII, in Sir Herbert Risley's work on the People of India.

Nothing is more striking in Mr. Chirol's volume than this Association of Political agitation with caste ambitions (p. 77). He insists that the spirit of revolt is combined with some of the most reactionary conceptions of authority that the East has ever produced—an almost unthinkable combination of spiritualistic idealism and of gross materialism, of asceticism and sensuousness, of overweening arrogance when it identifies the human self with the Universal self and of demoralising pessimism when it preaches that life itself is but a painful illusion.

Nevertheless, he wisely reminds us, Hinduism the name for a social religious system has for more than thirty centuries responded to the social and religious aspirations of a considerable fraction of the human race and represents a great and ancient civilisation. In his introduction Sir Arthur Lyall summarises the case to the same effect: "We have the strange spectacle in certain parts of India of a party capable of resorting to methods that are both reactionary and revolutionary of men who offer prayers and sacrifices to ferocious divinities and reverence the Government by seditious journalism, preaching primitive superstition in the very modern form of leading articles. The mixture of religion with politics has always produced a highly explosive compound especially in Asia."

The Indian leaders. or some of them, proclaim, on the other hand, that the commotion is innocent due to Brahminical reaction but is a normal movement forward. The foundation of Indian Society in all its phases, they contend, has been authority and its iron principle obedience to authority. What did we learn, they go on, from English literature and patriotism, nationality, freedom, in a word, emancipation. You suppose that ideas like these everyday common places with you must be universals. They were not always so with you. With you they are not so many centuries old. With us they are brand new, they are drawn from your great books just as Italians drew the Renaissance from the freshly recovered books of Greece and Rome.

What you call unrest is not political demoralisation though it produces a whole rash school of resentful iconoclasts just as the Italian Renaissance did or just as the German Reformation had to write the Anabaptists and the Peasant's Revolt. If it is not political demoralisation still less is it crafty religious reaction using the natural dislike of alienable. Unrest has spiritual inwardness that you ever try to understand and whatever else it is do not describe it as New Hinduism or Brahminical section. It is a strange medley of asceticism, self-restraint and the kind of patriotism that discovers in Indian faiths and letters finer and deeper sentiment and expression of sentiment, than all that is best in the sentiment of Europe. What is found in the Vedas exists nowhere else. The old fashioned, purely orthodox kind of community was not, Mr. Chirol conveys to you, affected by this. On the contrary, they constantly protested against the anti-English because of the English educated community. It is not they who investigated unrest though they may have indirectly aided it. They have slowly been converted to the new ideals and new effort. English thought is permeating India and has brought about a silent change in Hindu ideas which all the persecution of Mahomedan conquerors failed to effect. You have shown yourself less generous than the Moghuls and Pathans, though you are a more civilised dominant race than they were. Hindus who were willing to embrace Islam and to fall in with the Moslem regime became the equals of the dominant race. With you there has been no assimilation. You did not seek it, you repulsed it. The Indian mind is now set in a direction of its own. The reverence for authority is being discarded. In its place has come the duty of independent judgment in every sphere of thought; is it not that you sense too? Hence, disrespect for age, for immemorial custom, for political questions.

This is the frame of mind with which, in important parts of India, we have to deal, and it is just as well, in view of an approaching propaganda in this country that we should at least know something about it. Let us remember encouraging facts in the other side. We condemn our own system of education in India as too literary, as unbalanced, as non-religious, as non-moral. That it has done what was intended, nobody dreams of saying. That it has led to some results that nobody expected, is painfully true. But it is a mistake to regard it as all failure. After all, it has given us Indian Judges of the highest professional skill and of unimpeached probity. It has given us a host of officials of no mean order and some of them have risen high in the Service. The appointment of two Indian Members to the Council of the Secretary of State has shown their aptitude for important business and responsible deliberation.

There is no room here for trying to read all the signs in the Indian skies. Those who know best and latest believe that in spite of much to discourage there is more to encourage. With candour and patience in which even political parties do not always fail and that constancy in which nation never fails, we are justified in good hope for the years immediately before us. King Edward in his Proclamation of November, 1908, recounted how "difficulties such as attend all human rule in every age and place had risen up from day-to-day. They have been faced," he said, "by the servants of the British Crown with toil and courage and patience, with deep counsel and a resolution that has never faltered nor shaken. The Proclamation of the direct supremacy of the Crown sealed the unity of Indian Government and opened a new era. The journey was arduous, and the advance may have sometimes seemed slow but the incorporation of many strangely diversified communities under British guidance and control has proceeded steadfastly and without pause." The same course should enable our next descendants, too, to survey the Indian labours of the past "with clear gaze and good conscience," "I believe" said Mr. Bright in 1858, "that upon this question depends very much, for good or for evil the future of this country of which we are citizens and which we all regard and love so much."

INDEX.

Third Edition. 1,500 Copies. June 1920. G. A. Natesan & Co., Madras.